The Executive
Career Guide
for MBAs

The Executive Career Guide for MBAs

Inside Advice on Getting to the Top from Today's Business Leaders

Richard H. Beatty
Nicholas C. Burkholder

John Wiley & Sons, Inc.
New York • Chichester • Brisbane • Toronto • Singapore

Library of Congress Cataloging-in-Publication Data:

Beatty, Richard H., 1939–
    The executive career guide for MBAs : Inside advice on getting to
the top from today's business leaders / Richard H. Beatty, Nicholas
C. Burkholder.
      p.   cm.
    Includes bibliographical references
    ISBN 0-471-55709-9 (cloth : alk. paper)
    1. Management—Vocational guidance.   2. Executives—Recruiting.
I. Burkholder, Nicholas C. II. Title.
HD38.2.B42   1996
658.4'0023'73—dc20   95-17417

Printed in the United States of America

10 9 8 7 6 5 4 3 2 1

To those who aspire to positions of leadership in
these challenging and confusing times

PREFACE

A mighty maze! but not without a plan.

—Alexander Pope

As we approach the year 2000, business careers look tenuous at best. The restructuring ax continues to fall on middle managers who once felt secure in their positions. Employers offer no assurances that anyone's position is "safe" or that the ladder to better, more responsible jobs will be available. Hard work, long hours, the proper degrees, the right contacts—all have less power. The rules for executive success have changed in fundamental ways.

Millions of aspiring executives today find themselves bewildered and frustrated as they try to plan meaningful, satisfying careers and realize a sense of personal success in the quicksands of the new age of continuous change and organizational turmoil. With the advent of reengineering and sizable corporate downsizing, entire layers of management have been cut, and the old familiar pathways for career planning and growth, in many cases, are simply nonexistent.

Continuous change and career uncertainty are now the order of the day. Constantly changing ground rules coupled with increased competition in the job market for executives and managers have served to create a complex and frustrating maze for individuals seeking satisfying and rewarding careers. In the midst of this continuous turmoil, executives are searching for a piece of solid ground in which to drive their stake and anchor their sense of personal advancement and career success. This book provides the directions to that solid ground from which to build your executive career.

The maxim "Change is the only constant" has been repeated ad nauseam. Some managers and potential executives are reacting to this rate of change, to the lack of control and predictability, by going into a holding pattern. They are waiting for change to slow down or become more predictable. This is just the opposite of what they need to be doing. They've ceased making a contribution and stopped growing. They have delayed their own professional development, waiting for the definitive software package or management trend. This reaction represents the antithesis of what you should do to take control of your career and become even more productive.

There are no easy answers. There will always be new programs to learn and management techniques to consider. We are often overwhelmed by too much theory and a lack of facts, but our rate of learning continually increases as we get better at managing these kinds of changes. There are also, however, simple, lasting truths that can serve as guiding career principles. This book has identified those truths that will enable you to deal with the incredible challenges you will face.

This book provides a comprehensive plan for executive success in the new era. It reviews the fundamental changes now sweeping through American business, details the elements for executive success in that changing environment, and provides guidelines for a successful executive job search. It provides a comprehensive, thought-provoking plan for helping executives successfully negotiate the complex career maze now facing them, and offers an effective formula for restoring focus, order, and meaning to their business lives.

This book helps you negotiate that maze. It reviews the fundamental changes now sweeping through American business, details the elements for executive success in that changing environment, and provides guidelines for a successful executive job search. This book is about change. The criteria for success has changed. It is also about opportunity, which will belong to those who recognize and embrace the changes detailed here.

The fundamental definition of executive success has changed significantly. This book is based upon current research and testing. What were valid criteria for measuring executive success even two to three years ago no longer apply.

Today there is a whole new definition of executive success. Understanding the extent of this change and its significance from a personal development standpoint is paramount to achieving success in today's business environment. Without such understanding, executive careers will flounder.

What is meant by executive success today? How does one prepare for a successful career in the new business environment? This book provides timely answers to both of these important questions.

Chapters 1 through 3 are based on an extensive survey of over 3,000 top business schools' deans, placement professionals, executive recruiters, and corporate executives around the world. We solicited their views as to the following:

- Their definition of executive success and its essential components.
- The major challenges facing today's executives.
- Suggestions for current and aspiring executives.

Responses to this initial survey helped formulate a subsequent questionnaire for use in conducting more thorough, indepth surveys and interviews of some 429 key executives. Many of those interviewed spoke eloquently and sometimes passionately about addressing themselves to the skills, attitudes, and level of commitment required of executives in today's challenging business environment. This book is a direct result of those surveys and interviews, and is filled with direct quotes from many of these important respondents.

The findings were then further validated through lengthy personal interviews with highly regarded business leaders including two that are universally considered to be among the world's most respected and effective executives: James Burke, former Johnson & Johnson Chairman and John Bogle, Chairman of the Vanguard Group of Investment Companies. Their insights and wisdom regarding the measure of executive effectiveness enrich this volume in important ways.

The definition of executive success, emerging from this study, should help you clarify what is truly important today in attaining success in the modern business climate. Further, the definition should also serve as a constant beacon for career planning and personal development, allowing you to focus on selecting the positions and assignments that will help you to develop and refine those qualifications essential to long-term career success.

Noted journalist James Fallows (*Looking at the Sun,* Pantheon Books, New York, 1994, p. 452) has addressed Bernard Lewis's view that it is not, as many Americans think, "rot or loss of will" that explains the rise and fall of empires. Rather "their fatal defect was their inability to see or believe how the world had changed around them." As it is with empires, it is with organizations and individual careers. Although most American corporations have started to become more competitive, soon their only alternatives will be to flourish or perish as the challenges posed by Eastern Asia increase dramatically. There is a great deal at stake here and the benefits of success will be substantial.

Chapter 4, Managing a Successful Career, provides both the strategy and the day-to-day tactics that will enable you to attain your career goals. It contains numerous helpful suggestions for both planning and managing career success in the new business environment.

It is clear that in today's uncertain business environment, executives need to have well-tuned job-hunting skills if they are to succeed in realizing their career goals. The second half of the book—Chapters 5 through 12—deals with the topic of executive job search. It will help you develop the skills necessary to both identify and land the kinds of jobs that will be important to you in pursuing career success. Topics cover resume preparation, interviewing, networking, and the effective use of recruitment advertising and search firms. Much of what is covered here can be applied with equal effectiveness both inside and outside your current organization, as you pursue your career objectives.

Building on the extensive research behind the best selling books, *The Resume Kit, The Five Minute Interview, The Perfect Cover Letter, Get the Right Job in Sixty Days or Less,* and others, the reader is provided with a comprehensive, step-by-step process for conducting a successful job search. This process incorporates the research from the first half of the book, paying particular attention to ways to best package yourself based on the success attributes that organizations now value as important to executive effectiveness.

In both our research and writing, we have sought to provide a single source of clear, proven career advice that can be easily assimilated and put into action.

Now, as ever, fortune favors those who make their own luck. The information you need to make your own luck follows. We wish you great success.

RICHARD H. BEATTY
NICHOLAS C. BURKHOLDER

ACKNOWLEDGMENTS

This project owes a very special debt of gratitude to Jack Bogle and Jim Burke. Dean Keller's time and attention particularly at the beginning of this project were exceptionally helpful and will always be remembered. The book was enhanced immeasurably by the knowledge and skills of Dick Luecke. Mary Simon's persistence and professionalism in scheduling and conducting key interviews was vital to our success. And to Mike Hamilton—a special note of thanks.

RICHARD H. BEATTY
NICHOLAS C. BURKHOLDER

We are also grateful to the NorthStar Center for Career Development Professionals for conducting the surveys and analyzing the results. Their knowledge of career management trends and issues is unparalleled and was instrumental to the success of this project.

John and Paul, writers of distinction—for your most excellent example.

And Nancy, thank you for making sure I finished. I will be obliged in perpetuity.

N.C.B.

CONTENTS

1

THE CHANGING FACE OF AMERICAN BUSINESS

May you be cursed to live in interesting times.

—A Chinese saying

After decades of growth and prosperity, the managerial career has come under unprecedented attack. A Conference Board study estimates that between 1979 and 1987, more than a million managers and professional staff workers lost their jobs. Between 1982 and 1994, General Electric reduced its workforce from 400,000 to 220,000. Very few of those lost positions were blue-collar. Clerical, staff, and managerial personnel took most of the hit. During the recession of 1990 to 1992, an estimated 1.6 million jobs were lost, some 680,000 of them attributable to corporate restructuring. When the recession ended, an unusual thing happened: the big corporations didn't hire many people back, many just kept on cutting. Between 1993 and 1995, tens of thousands of additional positions have been eliminated. IBM has reduced their worldwide head count from

406,000 in 1985 to 235,000 today. AT&T, Sears, Kodak, and Procter & Gamble also reduced their total employees during the 1990s, accounting for well over 100,000 lost positions—many in the managerial ranks.

If you're planning to enter the managerial workforce—or if you are already a part of it—these are uncertain times. But they are also times of opportunity. The two usually go together. People hoping to enter the lower and middle ranks of management face the fact that demand is weak. Those already occupying these positions may find fewer opportunities for vertical mobility and face the ongoing threat of downsizing. Nevertheless, if you are thoughtful and savvy in how you present yourself and handle your career, you can have a satisfying and rewarding future in American business. As we will see later, the demand for managers cut in the traditional mold is smaller, but the demand for people with knowledge and a talent for getting things done is on the rise.

BUSINESS TODAY

To better prepare yourself for fulfilling your career aspirations, it is a good idea to review the present state of American business. American business is currently in an extended period of reformation and change. The painful personnel cutbacks just mentioned are one symptom; an unprecedented spate of alliances between traditional rivals, such as the Motorola-IBM-Apple venture to develop and manufacture the PowerPC chip, is another. How, or when, or if this period will end is unclear.

If you were around the business scene during the early 1980s, you might have sensed the beginnings of this reformation. United States firms were then clearly taking it on the chin from Asian competitors in industries such as consumer electronics, automobiles, steel, and memory chips. There was no mistaking that the world had changed, and that the glory days of unchallenged American industrial dominance were ending.

Some point to the publication of *In Search of Excellence* by Thomas Peters and Robert Waterman in 1981 as the firebell in the night that signaled to the American business community that change was both necessary and possible. Vincent Barabba describes this event:

> *In Search of Excellence* became a best-seller, inspired a PBS television series, and touched off much soul-searching and discussion in corporate offices large and small. In this sense, the book became something of a manifesto for the period of U.S. business reformation in which so many companies are now engaged. . . . Not coincidentally, the late 1970s and early 1980s witnessed a growing awareness of Japanese management techniques focusing on quality, continuous improvement, and customer satisfaction.[1]

Companies like Xerox, Motorola, and Ford were among the first to pick up the spirit of this movement. Hundreds of others followed. As Barabba makes clear, "the many Japanese management techniques that found their way to North America and Europe in the 1980s share two common understandings: first, that these processes have only one purpose: to satisfy customers and, second, that these processes have only one purpose: to satisfy customers." This approach and its adoption by forward thinking American companies, has been instrumental in shaping the business scene of the 1990s.

In retrospect, we can now see that the fundamental change in American business is taking place along six major fronts:

1. Attention to the primacy of the customer.
2. The drive to "reengineer" business processes.
3. Flatter organizational structures and a widespread use of self-managed teams.
4. Cross-functional integration of business activities.
5. An altered relationship between employees and employers.
6. Greater emphasis on innovation.

Your career in business will most likely be affected by one or more of these important developments.

The Primacy of the Customer

"Focus only on the customer, and everything else falls into its proper perspective and proper priority almost automatically." This was the advice of Chrysler chairman, Robert J. Eaton, in his 1993 letter to shareholders, and it says in a nutshell what more and more companies are thinking and acting on these days.

There is a growing recognition that all business activities must have a visible connection to serving the customer. All of the business improvement programs of the past decade (TQM, QFD, reengineering, etc.) take the customer as the starting point and work back into company activities, asking the question, How does this job, that job, moving an order form from clerk A to clerk B, add value for the customer? The object of these improvement programs is to eliminate those activities that cannot justify themselves as serving the customer.

This is threatening stuff—especially in staff jobs that have no contact or visible connection to customers. Everything now has to be justified in terms of the customer. Positions and activities cannot be supported because they have always existed on the organization chart. They need to demonstrate how they add value for customers.

Reengineering

Michael Hammer, perhaps one of the most sought-after management gurus of the early 1990s, has said that when people ask what he does for a living he tells them that he is "reversing the industrial revolution." The industrial revolution overturned what is called the craft system of manufacturing in favor of mass production and broke down the entire process of converting inputs to final output—a process completed by one or a few skilled craftsmen—into small, sequential steps. The mass production system was one of "small jobs for small people." Now, reengineering specialists like Hammer are working to change the system back to bigger, less defined jobs for "bigger" people.

As commonly practiced, reengineering takes customer satisfaction as the ultimate goal and organizes work and resources into processes that most effectively and economically meet that goal. This means more than simply finessing incremental improvements out of existing operations. It means creating optimal processes as if we were starting, as Hammer has said, "with a clean sheet of paper." In this scheme, no position is sacred. Anything that does not serve the goal of customer satisfaction—in terms of lower cost delivery, faster delivery, and so forth—can be cut.

Reengineering advocates promise reductions in costs and cycle time in the range of 50 to 75 percent. Early studies indicate a disparity between the promise and the reality of these programs, but while the jury may be out on the effectiveness of reengineering, companies will continue to scrutinize their core processes, searching for ways of improving delivery of products and services to customers. This concentration on processes is, in fact, a direct legacy of the quality movement. One of its spiritual leaders, W. Edwards Deming, cautioned executives to "manage the process and not the people." Underscoring the trend toward reengineering is a 1993 survey of Fortune 1000 companies by Mercer Management Consulting, which indicated that at least half of the companies planned to undertake some process reengineering over the following few years.

FLATTER ORGANIZATIONS AND SELF-MANAGED TEAMS

Middle managers have traditionally served as conduits for the flow of information and control between higher and lower levels within the corporation. Top management directives were passed down to lower levels through a succession of middle managers, who likewise saw to the implementation of those directives. Information and problems generated at the lower levels were analyzed and passed upward to higher management through this same system of conduits. This is the classic hierarchical organization, and it has undergone a substantial amount of waxing and waning during this century. In 1900, the typical business organization had just 3 levels of management; by the 1960s, this had grown to 13.

Corporations have come to recognize that multiple levels of management create both excessive cost and too much separation between the "thinking" and the "doing." It reserves for management the business of thinking and leaves the doing to the ordinary worker—as if those closest to the actual work are incapable of thoughtful contributions. As Steven Rayner has described it:

> Historically, corporations have limited employee involvement by narrowly defining jobs, filtering information, maintaining tight spans of control, and concentrating decision making, responsibility, and authority in the upper echelons of management. This approach to controlling the work behavior of employees is so pervasive that some experts have come to see it as a dominant management paradigm, one that directly affects how managers interact with members of the workforce.[2]

This is not a paradigm designed to get more than the minimum level of creative input from nonmanagerial personnel. Nor is it one that is likely to respond quickly to changing technology, changing customer requirements, and new competition.

To alter this paradigm, many corporations are adopting the simple but timeless principle of moving decision making to the lowest possible level—where it is nearest those doing the actual work. In the process, they are imploding their hierarchies to achieve flatter, leaner organizational units. They are effectively "delayering" their structures (see Figure 1–1). Throughout the developed world, organizations are scaling back their pyramids to as few as six levels, and some predict this number will be reduced to three by the end of this century. Consultant Dan Tobin describes the effect of this movement at one large manufacturer: "At Caterpiller's transmission unit only two levels of management now stand between the line worker and the unit general manager where

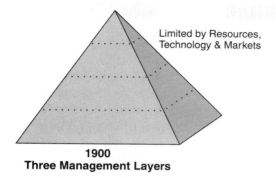

1900
Three Management Layers

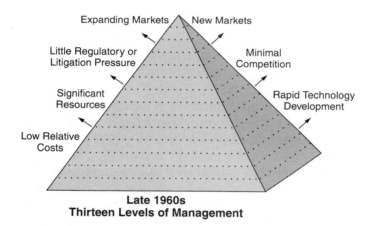

Late 1960s
Thirteen Levels of Management

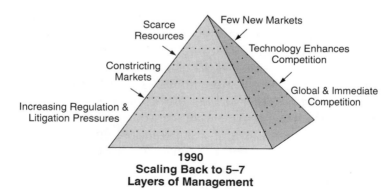

1990
Scaling Back to 5–7
Layers of Management

Figure 1–1   The Old and New Organizational Pyramids

once there were five. This elimination of managerial positions is widespread and bound to continue."[3]

In many instances, the work previously done by middle managers is being handled by self-managed teams. Teams eliminate the need for many managers and they alter the roles of those who remain from "boss" to "coach" or "teammate." Experienced managers have to learn to operate effectively in situations where they do not command authority; where they cannot exercise traditional control.

Today, an estimated ten million American workers are part of work teams and this number is expected to increase in the years ahead. Ninety percent of Corning employees are on teams. Honda uses teams at all organizational levels. And Xerox Canada develops all new products through teams.

Cross-Functional Integration

Ever since the development of the large industrial corporation, activities have been divided into specialized functions: marketing, manufacturing, finance, engineering, human resources, and so forth. Organizing by functions has been an effective way of breaking work into logical components, allowing people with specialized skills to apply themselves to those different tasks. It also fits neatly with the idea of the specialization of labor, the reigning philosophy of industry from the time of Adam Smith.

The weaknesses of this mode of organizing only became evident as companies grew larger. Departments found themselves quartered in separate buildings. Knowledge about processes, products, and customers became trapped within departments. Employees identified with their departments and viewed outsiders as competitors for scarce resources. For top managers, integration of separate efforts became difficult and time consuming and was often lost entirely.

Forty years ago, Peter Drucker described the worst features of the functional organization as, "[A]n organization of misunderstandings, feuds, empires and Berlin Wall building . . . [requiring] elaborate, expensive, and clumsy management crutches—coordinators, committees, meetings, troubleshooters, special dispatchers—which waste everybody's time without, as a rule, solving much." Many readers currently working in large functional organizations will recognize how little things have changed since Drucker first penned those words.

One of the important challenges for today's managers is to find ways to integrate the work of the different functional departments. Vince Barabba of General Motors Corporation has described this challenge as getting the different functional "silos" to share their expertise and knowledge in service of the larger corporate goals:

> There's the marketing silo, the finance silo, the engineering silo, and so on. Each has tremendous accumulated skills and specialized understandings about some aspect of our business and our market. Each has a critical piece of the knowledge and the know-how we need to fully understand and serve the modern automobile owner. The trouble is in linking together those critical pieces in ways that knowledge is shared and truly market-based decisions are made.[4]

Two approaches to achieving this "linking together" are (1) the use of cross-functional teams, and (2) reorganizing the activities of the corporation from vertical to horizontal structures.

The use of cross-functional teams has been a growing feature of American business and many point to the development of the highly successful Ford Taurus as a prime example of the benefit of their use. The new Taurus model, which was destined to become the best selling car in North America and save its builder from decline, was developed by a cross-functional team that drew the best people from all the relevant functional areas of the company: design, engineering, manufacturing, customer service, finance, and marketing. Knowledge was tapped from all the isolated pockets of the company, and new knowledge about customer needs and what would constitute a "best-in-class" automobile were developed through "Team Taurus."

The result was nothing short of astounding. The same designers, engineers, and assembly workers who had been building clunky, undistinguished automobiles under the acronym of F.O.R.D.—Fix Or Repair Daily—produced a vehicle that was stylistically and operationally a crowd pleaser. Today, virtually all new auto models produced in North America are the products of similar cross-functional team efforts. That model of product development is found in other industries in growing numbers.

Some companies have developed cross-functional teams to such an extent that virtually all personnel—from top to bottom—are involved on some project team at any given time. This fact underscores a new requirement for managers: that they be able to work effectively with people from many levels and from many disciplines.

The cross-functional project teams just described operate within the bounds of the traditional functionally organized company. Team members maintain their ties to particular departments. Some firms are attempting to hardwire cross-functional integration into the organization chart by redesigning themselves into what are called horizontal corporations. Unlike the traditional organization that is structured around functions or departments, the horizontal organization is designed around a handful of "core processes," such as new product development, sales and fulfillment, and customer support.[5] This is the reengineering process described earlier and seeks the same benefits: the elimination of non-value-adding activities; less operating costs; none of the "disconnects" that occur when work moves from one functional area to another—as it so often does in the traditional organization. Also eliminated, however, are a number of employment positions, including managerial ones. Walter Kiechel III put it bluntly in a Fortune article:

> Certainty: There will be fewer managers. It's not just that [information technology] is rendering obsolete their functions of gathering information and passing it up and down the hierarchy; they are being displaced by folks really deep into a particular skill or discipline . . .[6]

The mix of employees is also changing. If you are going to manage people, it is a good idea to know what kinds of people you will be dealing with. The Bureau of Labor Statistics (BLS) currently estimates that 25 percent of all the new jobs created between now and 2005 will fall into the "technical/professional" category. Sometimes we call these knowledge workers. The fastest growing category in the workforce is "technical/professional." (Many readers will fall into this category.) These people have loyalties to their "craft" and careers that supersede their loyalty to the corporation. They need to be managed in different ways.

Dealing with the Broken Social Compact

How many times have you heard this or something like it at a company meeting or read it in an annual report: "Our employees are our most valuable asset. We depend upon their skill, creativity, and commitment." Statements like this are now standard fare in corporate America and are undoubtedly delivered with a great deal of sincerity.

They are a part of an unwritten "social compact" between employer and employees in many companies. That compact implies a mutuality of interest, loyalty, and trust. Some companies actually take it seriously. As honorable as this may be, the "social compact" has been broken by many corporations, who seem to be among the last to recognize the breach. The evidence is in the massive layoffs mentioned earlier, and in growing evidence that layoffs continue even as these companies grow in output and profits.

Just about everyone now understands that we are expendable, and that few of us will spend a lifetime with one organization. Yet corporations expect (and need) the full cooperation, creative energy, and loyalty of their employees. In the spirit of what goes around comes around, these corporations may discover that their own lack of loyalty to employees may come back to haunt them in the form of a disloyal and demoralized work force. One of the challenges for managers today and the near future will be to engage the full capacity of their subordinates, many of whom will be as keen on "looking out for number one" as their employers have been in recent years.

Innovation

Peter Drucker once said that a business has two purposes: to innovate and to create a customer. Today, we see that the fates of enterprises and entire industries are often tied to their abilities to innovate in product development, service delivery, process improvement, and adoption of new technologies. James Utterback of MIT's Sloan Graduate School of Management has written recently,

> Innovation is at once the creator and destroyer of industries and corporations. Over the years, new technologies have made industrial giants out of many upstart firms, invigorated older ones that were receptive to change, and swept away those that were not. Today, when competitiveness hinges on the ability to develop or adapt new technologies in products, services, and processes, understanding the dynamics of industrial innovation and change is essential for survival and success.[7]

The ability to part with those familiar things that made them successful in the past and to innovate the products and services that will lead them into the future is the only way to survive and prosper in a fast-changing world. In high-technology industries in particular, the need to leap from one wave of technology to the next occurs at a brisk pace. Indeed, survival in these industries depends on it, reminding us of the expression, "When faced with a steamroller technology, you either become a part of the new technology or a part of the road."

Few companies develop the capacity for adapting to technological change over long periods of time. In fact, scholarly research would indicate that firms which dominate one generation of technology seldom maintain leadership in the next. We see this in the way IBM's unchallenged leadership in computers has been supplanted by new, formerly unknown companies: Dell and Compaq in personal computers; Cray and Thinking Machines in the field of super computing; Sun Microsystems and Hewlett Packard in the fast-growing workstation segment.

There are some corporations, however, that seem to keep pace with new technology and maintain leadership over long time spans. 3M, Corning, Johnson & Johnson, Hewlett Packard, Motorola, and General Electric come to mind as some of the more prominent ones. In the financial services industry, Goldman Sachs, Salomon Brothers, and Morgan Stanley stand out as firms that have innovated very well and very consistently. These, and firms like them, seem to have institutionalized a capability for innovation, as Drucker insisted that all firms must. The need for product and process innovation will continue apace in American business, and those managers who understand the dynamics of innovation and how to nurture it will be in high demand.

The kind of multiple transformations taking place in America's corporate giants is exemplified by the experience of Xerox Corporation beginning in the early 1980s.

Like many U.S. firms, Xerox learned and adopted the Japanese quality management methods—in its case, through direct exposure via its Japanese joint venture, Fuji Xerox. In early 1992, Xerox altered its organization structure, redefining its operations around fairly independent global business divisions. According to CEO Paul Allaire, "Xerox had all the structure, practices, and values of a classic big company. First, we were an extremely 'functional' organization . . . second, we were staff-driven."

Reorganization at Xerox aimed at making the $17 billion company more entrepreneurial, also more innovative and responsive to customers, technology, and competitive challenge. While the changes were aimed at the organizational architecture of the company, the greatest impact was to be felt in ranks of management, and in the managerial qualities that the company would need to reach its objectives. As Allaire told an interviewer from the *Harvard Business Review,* "We want people who can hold two things in their heads at the same time, who can think in terms of their individual organizations but also in terms of the company as a whole."[8] Xerox changed its compensation scheme for managers to motivate and reward this type of holistic behavior.

While Xerox exemplifies that change and reformation are taking place in American business, Allaire's comments speak to the talents that managers in general will need to have. But more on this later.

VISIONS OF THE FUTURE WORKPLACE

How the workplace in which you intend to spend your career will look has been the subject of both intensive study and creative imagining. Both help us understand the nature of managerial work in the future, the skills and competencies that will contribute to success, and how you need to think about managing your own career.

The U.S. Bureau of Labor Statistics (BLS), provides current and projected employment figures, both in the aggregate and in key occupational categories. Using a baseline of 1992, the BLS projects that the entire U.S. labor force will grow from 127 million to 150 million by the year 2005—a growth of 18 percent. Within the occupational categories that concern most readers, the outlook is surprisingly good. Growth in executive/managerial, specialized professional, technical, and marketing/sales employment is expected to outpace the rate of growth of overall employment, as summarized in Table 1–1. Administrative support and clerical positions, on the other hand, will fail to grow at this faster rate. The projected growth

Table 1–1   Projected U.S. Employment Growth, 1992–2005

Occupational Category	1992 (Millions)	2005 (Estimated Millions)	Change (in Percent)
Executive administrative, and managerial	12.0	15.2	27%
Professional specialty	16.6	22.8	37%
Technicians and related support	4.3	5.6	30%
Marketing and sales	12.9	15.6	21%
Administrative support, including clerical	22.3	25.4	14%

in executive, administrative and managerial positions should not stimulate false hopes, however.

Workplace 2000

A different vision of the near future workplace and the role of managers is provided in "Workplace 2000," a study done under the auspices of Cornell University's Center for Advanced Human Resources Studies.[9] This study brought together 57 carefully selected experts—corporate HR executives, academics, business consultants, government officials, and labor leaders—to create a collective picture of the world of work in the year 2000. These are among the important conclusions reached by the experts:

- There will be limited employment security and organization loyalty, yet work will be satisfying for most and productivity will be high.
- Top managers will reserve for themselves all decision-making authority on strategy and policy, yet expect a high commitment from employees, with high levels of quality, quantity, speed, and innovation.
- High levels of stress will prevail.
- Some 43 percent of support staffers will be less than full-time employees.
- Almost all executives and other managers will fill permanent, full-time positions.
- Organizations' structures will be markedly "flatter."
- Growth in head count will lag well behind growth in revenues and employee productivity.
- Professional/technical employment will increase to 43 percent—up from the current 33 percent in the experts' companies.
- A greater percentage of annual salary will vary with corporate performance.
- Employees will have to take greater responsibility for their own careers.

Workplace 2000 predictions underscore the importance of the recommendations you will find in this book. The workplace of the future promises to be every bit as unpredictable as it is in the present.

HANDY'S SHAMROCK

British scholar/author Charles Handy offers yet another vision of the future workplace: the "shamrock" organization. One leaf of the shamrock represents a small, permanent core of managers and technical professionals. According to Handy, this leaf contains the people essential to the enterprise. They are committed to the enterprise, and also dependent upon it.

Between them, says Handy, "they own the organizational knowledge which distinguishes that organization from its counterparts. Lose them and you lose the organization. . . . Organizations increasingly bind them to themselves with hoops of gold—with high salaries, fringe benefits, and German cars. In return, the organization demands of them hard work and long hours, commitment, and flexibility."[10]

The second leaf represents independent contractors, whose services are brought in as needed for special and recurring projects; it also represents the outside suppliers who perform activities once done by payroll employees. According to Handy, all nonessential work should be contracted out to others who make that work an essential specialty and, hopefully, do it better at lower cost. He points to the example of the New York Insurance Company, which ships its claims to Castle Island, Ireland, for processing "where the people are clever but also cheaper" than in the company's New Jersey claims facility.

The third leaf of the shamrock is a flexible labor force: part-timers and temps. This is, for better or worse, the fastest growing segment of the work force. One rationale for this flexible labor force is that so many firms are in service industries today. In fact, BLS projections show that service industries will account for almost all the growth in employment between 1992 and 2005. Unlike manufacturers, who can use slack periods to build inventory and do equipment maintenance, service companies cannot inventory their "products." This raises the question, Why have a permanent labor force at all times? Here, Handy's vision correlates with the Workplace 2000 vision of 43 percent contingent workers.

In Handy's shamrock, then, a minority of technical professionals and managers—well-educated knowledge workers—will have the only full-time jobs with a single organization. This is the traditional "job" model, but in Handy's world, it will be the exception and not the rule. A great number of others will be self-employed or employed in small supplier firms that sell their service to a variety of organizations. And there will be large groups of support personnel acting in part-time or temporary capacities.

This is a new model for business organization and one that challenges the traditional notion of lifetime employment, the managerial career, and the way managers will work. Together with the BLS and Workplace 2000 projections, it helps us form our own vision of how corporate managerial life will look and how we will work.

We have reviewed the key changes that have taken place in American business and discussed their implications for the work place and for how we operate in the present era. These changes center on making American businesses and the U.S. economy more competitive in the global marketplace. Increased international competition has been the impetus for many of the reformations described here.

While we may have started to turn the corner to competitiveness and stability, it is not the time to rest. International and particularly East Asian competition continues to grow. Recent economic downturns in Japan, for example, should not be mistaken for a decline in its competitiveness. Japan and the Pacific Rim in general will continue to become more formidable contenders in the world economy. Journalist and Japan/ East Asian expert James Fallows notes:

The success of the Asian system as a whole now poses a challenge to Western nations. At the end of the twentieth century, the world faces the possibility of mutual enrichment—financial, cultural, scientific, human—of a kind unimaginable during the era of colonial expansion and through the Cold War. Yet the terms of this new interaction will vary tremendously with the strengths and knowledge of each participant. People in each society, and societies as a whole, will end up either winners or losers, depending on how well they can adapt to the world's new rules. The adaptability of Western societies will depend on whether they can bring themselves, as did the nineteenth-century Japanese, to learn everything they can about powerful new systems and change their own practices where necessary—or whether, like the Chinese of the same era, they deal with unsettling new evidence by wishing it away.

The firebell has not grown silent. In pursuing a management career, you will be assured of one thing: interesting times.

2

THE SUCCESS ABSOLUTE

No one can guarantee success . . . only deserve it.

Winston Churchill

The changes sweeping American business, as described in the previous chapter, cannot help but alter our traditional notion of managerial work. These are, to use Dickens's words, "the best of times and the worst of times." If you are a management consultant, these are the best of times—reengineering is practically a full employment act for consultants; but to the thousands of employees on the receiving end of downsizing and reengineering projects, these are the worst of times; the very term "reengineering" has become a euphemism for unemployment.

Also deeply affected by these changes is our notion of success and career. This is what we explore in this chapter. Success, in the context of a changing world, must be redefined. No longer are the criteria of the past and the traditional ideas about career trajectories applicable. Not only will expectations have to be adjusted, but our sights will have to be reset and adjusted to accommodate the changing workplace.

In the following sections, we will examine these two key and interrelated concepts—success and career. We will redefine the notion of success from the perspective of the corporation and from the perspective of the individual executive. As an aid to seeing the corporate perspective, this chapter presents a set of challenges that executives of the present and future are expected to face. Career success depends upon the capacity of the executive to creatively and unflinchingly meet these challenges. We present comments and suggestions from top executives who were asked to address these issues.

SUCCESS IN THE CORPORATE PYRAMID

During most of the post-war era, growth was the primary goal of American corporations, and many were successful in that pursuit. Growth meant expansion of current business, new divisions, larger employment rolls, and, with these, an expanding management pyramid. Corporations could absorb large numbers of educated and ambitious people into their management ranks, and business careers flourished. Success meant landing a job with a good company after graduating from a good school, latching onto the right mentor—i.e., someone who was "on the move"—putting in the hours, and working one's way up the corporate career ladder.

With as many as thirty-six levels of management in some large firms, there were many rungs on the ladder to be climbed, each offering more responsibility, greater status, and higher compensation. In the heyday of the British Empire, young naval officers hoped for an occasional "short war and a sickly season" to cull the upper ranks and provide spaces for their own advancements. In post-war U.S. business, growth and normal attrition sufficed to a create a "demand pull" for junior managers and professional functionaries. There were always plenty of slots to be filled.

Success in the past required a combination of genuine merit and political acumen. Indeed, the cynical adage, "it isn't what you know, it's who you know" resonated in typical corporate settings of the past. Political savvy was at least as important as technical know-how and personal productivity where promotions were concerned, and a great deal of talent never surfaced or, at the very least, failed to flourish. Anyone who has labored in the traditional management pyramid for long understands this.

It should not be surprising that advancement was not entirely based on merit, since performance within bureaucracies is difficult to measure. The manager/bureaucrat's contribution to measurable business outcomes is often a matter of speculation as it is disconnected from the customer-serving processes of the organization. And in the absence of meaningful performance measures, seniority, ability to "get along" with others, number of people under one's supervision, and other factors naturally become the basis for advancement and rewards.

Certainly none of this suggests that those who have made it to the top of major corporations have not had talent, knowledge, and vision. The pathways to the very top have always been demanding. But there has been a much greater margin for error and mediocrity. The many layers of management that were common in the past provided plenty of room for "dead wood" and for superfluous functionaries.

The success absolute in this environment was showing up on time, putting in long hours, and "pleasing your boss."

A NEW DEFINITION OF SUCCESS

Today, the markets serviced by many of America's largest corporations have ended their headlong growth. Motor vehicle markets are a good example. They have slowed the year-on-year increases of industry unit sales with the saturation of two-car households and longer vehicle lives. To make matters more difficult for producers, these markets have been invaded by capable new competitors from abroad. Who in 1970, for example, would have guessed that names like Honda, Mazda, or Toyota would have provided formidable competition to Detroit's Big Three auto makers?

To maintain market share, producers in most industries today must be more agile in responding to demand and technological change. They must be faster in developing and bringing new models and products to market. Delivery of world-class quality at a reasonable price is becoming viewed as a "minimal" requirement.

These challenges cannot be met if a firm has to carry legions of unproductive managers, analysts, and staff personnel on its back. Everyone who draws a paycheck—from the lowest level production worker to the top executives—must measurably add to the ultimate goal of customer satisfaction. Even in industries such as telecommunications and computers, where growth continues apace, intensive competitive pressures have required that producer firms become lean and mean.

In industries generally, career ladders have been compressed or eliminated outright, providing fewer opportunities for promotion. Compensation increases and frequencies have tapered off. This fact requires some rethinking on the part of job seekers. Drucker once commented that few Americans are prepared to recognize this new reality. "When they prepare their resumes, they still try to list positions like steps up a ladder. It is time to give up thinking of jobs or career paths as we once did and think in terms of taking on assignments one after the other."[1]

Given the changing face of American business, we can articulate a new success absolute for the executive working within the corporation. That success absolute is: Do more, better, faster, with less. American business needs to get more results, faster, with far fewer resources. As an executive, you will be required to either fulfill that need or find some other vocation.

WHAT COMPANIES ARE LOOKING FOR

Given the new success absolute of do more, better, faster, with less, employers are looking for people capable of doing just that. Companies want "out-of-the-box" thinkers—men and women who not only add but create value for the company and thereby sharpen its competitive edge. They want to hire people who can make real contributions to the organization right away. These people, the right people for the job, are individuals who have vision and can make hard decisions. They are more inclined to direct the future than to stand by and watch it happen.

There is little or no room, particularly at the upper management levels, for people with a wait-and-see mentality. Successful executives take a broad view of their skills and goals. They are able to extrapolate from particular learning situations and apply their knowledge to other situations. They combine their knowledge with an encompassing understanding of the world around them and are able to maximize career potential and opportunities.

THE CHALLENGES OF ORGANIZATIONAL SUCCESS

So far, we've offered ideas about the need for a general reorientation to the world of business and to corporate career expectations. This reorientation sets the stage for a successful career in the competitive global economy. We now examine the problems executives will face in their day-to-day work lives, the very challenges you must be prepared to tackle and overcome.

Out of survey data gathered for this book emerged ten of the most critical challenges executives will be and are being faced with. These challenges are overarching in scope and crosscut virtually every industry. Every manager and executive can plan on confronting these issues to some degree at some point in his or her career.

1. *Adapting to an unprecedented and increasing rate of change.* Rapid change affects numerous aspects of business operations. Change has technological, demographic, political, economic, and environmental dimensions that executives need to understand. "We live in a world where change is the only constant," says Thomas F. Keller, Dean of Duke University's Fuqua School of Business.

Throughout history, those who have created or mastered change are the individuals who founded or shaped new industries: Thomas Edison and electric lighting; John Sears and mass merchandising; Henry Ford's innovation in production methods; Alfred Sloan and the mastery of multidivisional organization; Shewhart, Deming and Juran, whose ideas created the worldwide quality movement. These individuals were change-makers and change-masters and they enjoyed great success. Those who have failed to deal head-on with change have ended in the dustbin of history.

Historian Arnold Toynbee postulated that the fate of civilizations (and nations) was determined through a "challenge and response" mechanism. When changes occurred that presented a challenge or threat, it was the responsibility of the leadership to respond. Those civilizations whose leaders responded in creative and appropriate ways survived and flourished, while those that failed to respond properly fell into decline. Corporate leaders are under the same obligation to recognize challenges in their environments and to respond in appropriate ways. This is what being a change-master is all about.

At a minimum, every executive must understand that the world is dynamic, while institutions are slow to change, always lagging behind trends and changing realities. Left to their own devices, institutions such as corporations will not change, but will become relics—lifeless museum pieces. They need to be shoved. It is not the job of corporate executives to be curators or defenders of the way things are done.

Instead, the executive's job is to recognize when change is imperative or inevitable, to challenge the status quo, to develop realistic visions of the future and the strategies that will lead their companies to them. As John Maynard Keynes once told a critic: "When the facts change, I change. What do you do, sir?"

There is an important "people" component to the business of change. The messengers of change—the people with ideas that challenge the status quo—are often those we want least to hear from. Yet it is the executive's business to listen for them. Sociologist Lewis Coser described people with new ideas as "those who think otherwise, the disturbers of the intellectual peace." Business writer Richard Luecke describes these provocateurs for change as almost always being "outsiders." "They are the people who make us angry and uncomfortable with their methods, and our instinct is to ignore or to get rid of them."[2] Tom Peters's advice to CEOs is to act against this instinct, and he offers this contrary suggestion: "Within the next 12 months, promote to a position of significant responsibility at least one rabble rouser who doesn't like you or agree with you (on much of anything)."[3]

2. *Changing demographics and human resource management.* During the 1980s, there was a growing recognition that corporate success depended on people. People became "resources" and personnel administration departments became human resources management departments. Quality circles, participative management initiatives and other programs provided visible and measurable evidence that employees at all levels are capable of offering more than just a "day's work." Managers now recognize that they themselves don't always know best—instead, it is the people closest to the work who are usually the best resource for developing process improvement.

Unused or underutilized potential of people in the workplace can be crippling both to the workers in question and to the company. It is common knowledge that in most cases personnel—people—constitute the largest portion of operating expenses. Untapped potential is extremely wasteful—a liability to the company. The executive must become expert at drawing out the potential of others and at helping individuals take responsibility for developing themselves. Developing effective people skills is the first step toward increasing productivity. Without people who are able and willing to produce, all other efforts at increasing productivity will be ineffective.

A productive environment can occur only in a corporate culture that promotes a sense of trust and respect for divergent and diverse viewpoints. Employees who fear repercussions if they speak their minds or offer criticism are likely to keep their mouths closed—except when the boss's back is turned. Bosses who are willing to hear only they want to hear will miss out on finding out what they need to hear. It could be a very costly omission.

Thomas Keller adds: "Employees must feel secure if such an environment is to exist. In the perceived absence of such an environment, executives get nothing new—and not what they need."

The late W. Edwards Deming, who taught most of the industrial world the principles of effective quality management, said something similar when he insisted that corporations "drive fear from the workplace."

Changing demographic trends, growing cultural diversity in the population, a shrinking labor pool, and rigorous competition to attract well-educated, motivated, and qualified people have spurred additional innovations in human resource management. Executives will find themselves increasingly involved in efforts to improve the education and skill levels among the pool of potential employees. This will mean working through community outreach and training initiatives—particularly on behalf of traditionally underachieving groups. The importance of this issue was perhaps best addressed by Isaac Asimov at an Employment Management Association Conference in 1987. "You should reach out to the young and disadvantaged because it is right," Asimov said. "And what is right ultimately makes good business sense. So if you don't want to do it just because it is right, do it because it makes good business sense. And if you don't do it because it is right or because it makes good business sense, do it because you'll either have to or regret not doing so."

3. *Staying ahead of customer needs.* It used to be enough for companies to give customers what they wanted. Customer focus and sensitivity to their needs are "critical success factors," according to W. J. Delayo, vice president and chief financial officer for the Lander Company. Indeed, determining and fulfilling the needs of customers is the embodiment of the marketing concept to which all thoughtful business leaders and scholars now adhere.

Many successful executives have adopted a "customer orientation" approach toward not only the end-users of their company's products or services, but toward their staff and subordinates and anyone else they may come into contact with in a business capacity. A customer orientation provides the conceptual framework for improving people skills. "My business absolute is delighting the customer," says Shelly Carpenter, human resources director for Johnson & Johnson's World

Headquarters. One of the most successful Americans in Japan, Thomas J. Nevins, managing director of THT puts it this way: "A company must serve a great need, perform a great service, not for owners but for customers. When it turns its back on the customer, it ceases to be profitable. It ceases to exist."

Companies must also anticipate customer needs, impossible though this may seem. Peter Drucker once made the observation that "one can use market research only on what is already in the market." Nevertheless, Sony gave us the Walkman, Chrysler developed the wildly successful minivan, Japanese electronics firms offered up the facsimile machine, and Motorola and others have created an entire new industry based on pagers and cellular communications. None of these product concepts existed in the market before their producers anticipated customer needs and created them. Precious few consumers would have been able to articulate these products among their "needs" before the fact.

It is in the nature of being an executive to deal in the realm of ambiguity and uncertainty, occasionally placing major "bets" on new product concepts that few—even your current customers—have anticipated.

4. *Contending with the information explosion.* Ours is truly an information age. The downward slope in the cost of computing and memory power has resulted in an avalanche of information about buying patterns, customer profiles, manufacturing cost behaviors, and so on.

Today, point-of-sale information technology makes it possible for retailers to know exactly what is selling, the profit margin on a given foot of store shelf space, and how much they need to reorder from manufacturers at the end of each day. Direct-mail merchandisers are using information to better target potential customers for specific goods. Manufacturing managers use information technology to track and control costs at each work station. E-mail links employees in different functions together.

As recently as 1988, Peter Drucker was predicting an information-based organization. ". . . The typical organization will be knowledge-based, an organization composed largely of specialists who direct and discipline their own performance through organized feedback from colleagues, customers, and headquarters."[4]

This has happened faster than anyone imagined, but it has also created a downside that few imagined: We are being pummelled by data, information, and new knowledge—often to the point of overload. While it is incumbent upon executives to stay informed, they face a growing problem of separating what is important from "noise." We are reminded here of a CEO whose firm implemented E-mail. Naturally, everyone felt obliged to "copy" the boss with every memo. At first, this CEO had his secretary organize these memos for his evening reading. Eventually, he found himself buried in meaningless memos and took himself off the E-mail system entirely.

The executive must read, listen, and observe continually. The antennae have to be tuned in. Though it is necessary at times to be selective, it is even more crucial than ever before to be in direct communication with the frontline people in your operation.

5. *Instilling loyalty in employees.* Loyalty issues are extremely important. Loyalty once came with the job, and it was a two-sided arrangement. The unwritten "social compact" described in the previous chapter was that the company would provide long-term employment and the employee would give his or her loyalty. But layoffs, plant closings, and restructurings have rent the fabric of this compact. Workers stung by these upheavals can hardly be expected to maintain a commitment to an employer, and forecasters predict the average worker will change careers at least six times in the course of a working life. So what is the basis of mutual loyalty?

The environment today is much more quid pro quo; there must be a mutuality of interest, where value is traded for value. Executives must ensure employees value if they expect to receive value in return. "All success is based on agreement," points out Thomas J. Nevins, from Tokyo. "If colleagues don't agree or believe our work has value, we won't get very far. Realize that people will grant our requests when those requests appeal to their self-interest. They will give you what you want. But you must give first."

Since companies can no longer offer lifetime employment, they must offer something else. Just as executives must redefine their careers and assess their own employability, they must also consider the same issues for their employees. The security of lifelong employment must be replaced with the security of transferable and employable skills and expanding knowledge base.

6. *Managing scarcity while increasing productivity.* This is a new challenge for the American executive. Scarcity of capital, labor, and materials was seldom an important issue until recently. And until the 1980s, the minuscule growth in productivity in U.S. industry compared to major competing economies was largely ignored. Productivity in the growing service economy has hardly budged at all.

Today, input scarcity and the need to increase productivity in manufacturing and services are both recognized as serious challenges. And solving the productivity problem is viewed as the best solution to the problem of resource scarcity. This twin challenge is directly related to the new success absolute of doing more, better, faster, with less. During the 1980s, American corporations managed to increase manufacturing productivity and make more efficient use of resources while delivering higher quality output. Continuing that progress and extending it into the vast service economy will remain a challenge to executives of this decade and the next.

7. *Bringing more diversity into management ranks.* Issues of cultural and ethnic identity are becoming increasingly important in the United States and in the world, and business leaders must be sensitive to these issues. The United States is far more progressive than most other industrialized nations in this era. However, there is much work to be done toward incorporating diversity into American management. The makeup of American management must begin to reflect the demographics of the work force and the general population. It is

important as a way to stay abreast of customer wishes and needs. Management needs people who understand the pluralism and dynamism of the marketplace. Diverse perspectives are needed to effectively work in an increasingly complex society. "We can't afford to be managed by people with a 'one-world' view anymore," urges John DePalo, manager of human resources at Cooper's & Lybrand in Washington, D.C. "We actively need diversity."

The principles of equal opportunity regardless of subjective characteristics, such as ethnic identification, religion, race, or gender, must be effectively and fairly implemented. Fair and equitable promotion policies must be instituted that are above reproach. Performance, potential, ability, and drive must be among the objective criteria by which a managerial team, or a workforce, is built.

8. *Developing community and government relationships.* Companies are beginning to recognize the growing interdependence between themselves and communities. Partnerships with communities and government are on the rise. Businesses are forging these alliances to provide training and work programs, scholarship programs, and grants to retrofit companies with new technology, research assistance, and the like. Business executives are uniquely positioned to foresee the needs of the future and are called on to lead the way in these initiatives.

The health care crisis pales in comparison to the task of equipping our youth with skills and training that will ensure their employability as well as a competitive American work force. The nation's education system is not working. Business leaders must play a key role in helping government and communities provide appropriate training and career advice for the workers of the future. Fortunately some executives have started to work on the problem. Hoescht Celanese's Betty Dickey created a school-business partnership program for the Charlotte-Mecklenburg School District that is now a national model. Mike Wilson, advertising director for *The Wall Street Journal,* and School Match founder Dr. Bill Bainbridge put such programs on the national agenda when they forged *The Wall Street Journal*-Employment Management Association Foundation School Business Partnership Awards Program. Computer-World vice president John Corrigan has been a catalyst in bringing academicians in information systems and executives together, as well as arranging for replaced computer equipment to be donated to schools.

Business leaders must also be prepared to become active in community service programs and in issues of environmental quality. "Businesses need to accept the responsibility and commitment to make positive change in the community," advises Evelyne Steward, vice president of human resources at the Calvert Group.

These are tall orders and may seem far afield from the business of running a corporation. But community and government relations have become a part of doing business in a world where Newton's law is never far off. Corporate responsibility makes good business sense. And it is truly an area where each one of us can make a difference.

9. *Doing business in a litigious society.* The cost of legal fees and settlements continues to rise dramatically for American businesses. Increasingly, the courts are the venue for settling disputes of all descriptions. Few companies can afford either the expenses of legal actions or the wounds to public image and trust that typically accompany legal actions.

Although individual consumers and businesses would benefit greatly, we are not likely to see real tort reform this decade. As lawyers continue to popularize their trade, business leaders can expect an increase in the number of resource-consuming legal documents crossing their desks. Business executives in their strategizing and decision making need to be able to foresee possible legal ramifications for a particular course of action.

10. *Accepting risks and losses in order to attain long-term goals.* American business has been roundly criticized for being short-term oriented. Middle managers who are judged on

quarterly and annual results, and who move rapidly from assignment to assignment, naturally maximize the short-run and leave long-term outcomes to those who succeed them. Senior executives, in turn, are often driven by the same need to turn in good quarterly and annual results. The monkey on their backs, according to Michael Jacobs, author of *Short Term America*[5] is the set of institutional investors who own most of the shares of large public corporations. These investors—or, more correctly, the money managers who work for them—in turn are highly sensitive to share price fluctuations and quarterly results and do "the Wall Street walk" (sell the shares) at the first scent of trouble.

However, strong companies are built upon commitments to long-term goals, and these commitments may well follow a rocky and risky road in the short term. Executives have the daunting challenge of steering a steady course to long-term goals in the face of the myopic view of shareholders and even directors. "Enhance the long-term viability of the enterprise—resist the short-term scorecard in a manner which balances short- and long-term interests," advises Maureen McNulty, director of the MBA Career Management Center at Stanford University's Graduate School of Business.

Executives must find creative ways to balance long and short-term interests. Sacrifices of short-term profits may be acceptable if these sacrifices are part of a long-term plan or vision. Executive creativity is essential here. Sound planning based on broad understanding of the issues and a clear vision can go a long way toward steadying skittish investors and directors.

The challenges outlined here must be faced by virtually every executive. Your success in finding and holding an executive position will be greatly influenced by your ability to respond to them effectively. There are no clear guidelines for responding to them, but dealing with uncertainty and ambiguity is part of what being an executive is all about. In the following pages, we hope to be more explicit about how executives and aspiring executives can negotiate this rocky terrain successfully.

NEW MEASURES OF PERSONAL SUCCESS: CAPABILITIES AND PERFORMANCE

If the corporation has a new success absolute by which you will be judged—to do more, better, faster, with less—then you need to have your own personal definition of success. Ideally, the two definitions will be compatible.

The need to have your own notions of success is dictated by the fact that we can no longer depend on any particular company to provide long-term employment, career paths, and rewards. Personal definitions of success in the past were frequently related to job security (guaranteed longevity) and timely promotions up the corporate hierarchy. Other aspects of job and work-related satisfaction have not been thoroughly explored, nor in fact have they been considered important. Personal satisfaction has had little bearing on the concept of a management career. You went to work, you did your job, you waited to be promoted. In a sense, you delayed gratification by placing all criteria for success in the climb up the ladder. Consequently, those on the management career track had wrapped themselves tightly in the mantle of their positions.

Managers were their work. One's sense of self was virtually inseparable from vocation. As more and more women entered the professional ranks, they, too, were absorbed by the demands of the old corporate system, although they have been, as a group, better insulated against the I-am-what-I-do affliction.

The linkage of self-worth with career success remained relatively unproblematic as long as corporations could provide opportunities for advancement and as long as the "social compact" between corporations and their employees was maintained. But in the age of flat organizations and massive layoffs, careerists must redefine their own concept of success—that is, to "get a life."

Business professionals must look at how they can wrest satisfaction and meaning from something other than a title, a corner office, or frequent pay increases. All of these things can be arbitrarily snatched away, leaving the individual with nothing but a damaged ego. Today, success must be measured by internally generated criteria that become part of an individual's portfolio of skills and accomplishments: the design of a new product, the mastery of a more effective information system, a growing ability to motivate and mentor others, and so forth. These are things that cannot be removed by a reengineering consultant. They are satisfactions that we can carry with us all through our careers—careers that we control and manage.

If further persuading is necessary on this point, remember that few of us will have lifetime careers with any one company. There is no shortage of experts to tell us that we, unlike our parents, will have many careers with many companies. The old, stable world our parents knew is fast becoming a quaint memory. Charles Handy experienced this shift first hand, and describes it in this appealing story:

> Thirty years ago I started work in a world-famous multinational company. By way of encouragement, my employers produced an outline of my future career. "This will be your life," they said, "with titles and likely jobs." The outline ended . . . with myself as chief executive of a particular company in a particular far off country. . . . I left them long before I reached the heights they planned for me, and by then I knew that not only did the job they had picked out no longer exist, neither did the company I would have directed nor even the country in which I was to have operated.

Because companies may come and go, we must look to our own lives and personally managed careers for a sense of permanence and satisfaction. Several of the experts interviewed for this book have contributed their ideas about the meaning of personal success and how you can distinguish yourself from other job-seekers. "Redefine success," urges one corporate executive. "It is a different world now. Do not judge yourself by others that precede you. There are fewer top slots and the competition for them is much greater. Define your success by standards that you can control and attain. Be concerned with employability and contributions. Period." You also must educate your significant others regarding these new realities, too. Otherwise their expectations of you may be based on standards of another time that are no longer attainable.

Here it may be useful to again return to the notion of Handy's "shamrock" organization described in the previous chapter. The shamrock has a core of fairly permanent managers and professionals. It also has another leaf, a "contractual fringe" of individuals and organizations that do the outsourced work of the shamrock as needed. These organizations will undoubtedly have their own cores and fringes in turn. We can already see this model at work in firms like Chrysler Corporation and Reebok, where fairly small cores of employees manage allied supplier firms in creating big firm outputs. Xerox Corporation is also moving toward this model, having recently outsourced its considerable information activities to an outside firm, EDS.

The point for current and aspiring executives to consider is this: Your career will most likely move you from organization to organization, perhaps from one set of activities to something quite different. You will doubtless have to satisfy the success definitions of those various organizations, but because they are ephemeral and you are permanent (in your own terms), it is imperative that you articulate and satisfy your own success absolute. As Lau-tzu cautioned us, "Care about other people's approval and you will be their prisoner." If your personal success absolute hinges completely on the organization's particularities, its culture and structural turbulence, then you risk stultifying your career and personal growth.

Perhaps the common points on which both organizations and individuals can settle have to do with capabilities and performance. Performance is the measure of success, and performance is measured in results. An individual must bring to the table capabilities that the enterprise needs to do its job. And then he or she has to use those capabilities to good effect. Having brains or talent is insufficient. Being able to put them to use and show results is what ultimately counts.

Challenges of the job may be viewed as opportunities for developing one's capabilities. Performance may be viewed as a way to articulate one's capabilities. Then, if capabilities and performance are points of interface between the company and the individual, then both can be winners for however long the relationship lasts.

DEVELOPING YOUR CAPABILITIES AND BRINGING THESE TO FRUITION ON THE JOB

Capabilities and performance, then, should be measures for your own success absolute. Career growth, too, may now be measured in terms of increasing capabilities and a solid record of performance. Individuals can view their work, not so much as means to ends or means to ladder climbing, but as opportunities—opportunities for developing existing skills and expertise in functional areas and gaining exposure to new skills and knowledge of functional areas. Career success is defined as a matrix of capabilities and performance, and is something enduring. Your capabilities and performance record are transferable to other job situations. They are not subject to the vicissitudes of economic and business climates, nor are they lost when a company downsizes or when a position is eliminated.

What kinds of capabilities and performance standards should you expect to develop as a successful executive? William A. Dittmore, director of recruitment and college relations at General Mills notes: "Key words for the future are: Innovation, Speed, Commitment." And Peter A. Topping, director of graduate placement at the University of North Carolina's Flagler Business School says: "The combination of vision, understanding the need for change, and people skills is my formula for success."

To summarize, there is both an organizational and personal concept of success. Before you consider working for a corporation, make it your business to determine that firm's concept of success and how you will be measured against it. Ask yourself if this concept is compatible with your concept of personal success. Is there a serious conflict?

This assumes, of course, that you have developed your own success absolute. If you haven't already done so, this is the time to work on it. How do you define success? Is it salary, position, titles? Or is it a set of potentials, skills, and accomplishments?

The foregoing comments should serve as guidelines for how you might begin to think about your personal definition of success and about gaining control over your business career. They also introduce you to the next chapter, where we go into the components or elements of executive success that have been identified through our survey data and executive interviews.

In what follows, we lay out several criteria of executive success as identified by prominent executives, along with their advice on how to achieve success. Understanding these success "elements" will help you to define your own success absolutes, to develop your career goals. These essential elements are character, vision, leadership, quality, functional expertise, and productivity. These elements also suggest present and future trends in business that will have a direct bearing on your chances of achieving success in your field.

As you go through the next chapter, begin to think about how you are currently developing these areas, how you might change how you work to enable their development, and ways to incorporate them into a career plan.

3

THE ELEMENTS OF
EXECUTIVE SUCCESS

Fortune favors the prepared mind.

Thomas A. Edison

What is the alchemy of success for business executives? Why do some individuals enjoy careers that progress over the years, growing in responsibility and accomplishment, while others either fail or make little headway? Cynics point to knowing the right people and being at the right place at the right time. And to a certain extent they are right. We all know instances in which fortuitous events or connections have led to beneficial outcomes, perhaps even for ourselves. But these are not career-builders; they do not explain achievement over time.

Something else separates the great from the also-ran. This chapter presents those personal characteristics identified through survey research that are associated with executive success. Our survey is based on a comprehensive survey of over 3,000 executives, executives recruiters, and business school leaders. The survey responses were used to develop an in-depth questionnaire that we used to further survey or interview 429 key executives. Finally we conducted intensive interviews with 10 to 12 executives in a variety of industries. In each case, the interviewees were asked to identify the characteristics common to successful executives.

Based on our data, we have identified and defined six essential elements of executive success: character, vision, leadership, quality, functional expertise, and productivity. The first three areas—character, vision, and leadership—are largely issues of personal development. They address qualities of the individual that executives feel are fundamental criteria for success. The final three elements—quality, functional business expertise, and productivity—are related to skill areas in management and business.

Naturally, there is overlap between these two sets of characteristics. Areas of personal development frequently have a bearing on the development of skill areas, and achievement in skill areas will be reflected in areas of personal development as well. But for the sake of clarity, we have elected to separate these six areas into the two subdivisions of personal development and skill development. However, it should be remembered that there is a meaningful interplay between them, just as there is an interplay between our inner and outer lives, between what we think and what we do, between how we see things and what we see, between our view of ourselves and our view of others.

This division of "inner" and "outer" realms is more than a methodological device, however. It helps illustrate the conceptual shift we are advocating with respect to the definition of success. Personal success is today much more dependent upon characteristics and qualities of particular individuals— qualities generated within the person as opposed to expectations generated from an external source. In the past, personal success was largely dependent upon image management. Individuals who could fit into the mold of the corporate man (in the early days, it was indeed an arena almost exclusively of and for men) would be successful as members of the corporate bureaucratic structure. Success was driven by outer criteria—that is, fitting into the corporate bureaucracy, doing what you were told, meeting the right people, joining the right clubs, wearing the right suits, and so forth. Success was a function of fitting into and learning the ropes of an already existing system.

"The real issue of success strips down to what is underneath; that's what really matters," suggests Thomas Keller. "Executive success is dependent upon having a firm vision, a firm set of values, and a strong, realistic sense of self," he concludes.

Success now, as was discussed in the preceding chapters, is no longer so much about structure, but about substance. Today companies value capabilities that translate directly into measurable results. The development of each of these six areas is important for success. Executives we talked with stressed this fact. So while the areas may differ in relative weight or priority as prerequisites of success, and readers may rank them differently, it is through the combination of characteristics and attributes that the conditions of success are brought about or executed.

The presentation of success elements here is not in any rank order. In fact, the development of these areas occurs simultaneously, but unevenly, depending upon the age, experience, and career stage of the individual. A theme we continually return to is that what matters today are real contributions and real skills.

CHARACTER

Character is usually understood to be the sum of individual traits: courage, discipline, integrity, honesty, perseverance, and so forth. In the world of business, character includes the willingness to accept short-term costs for the benefit of the long term. Character is tempered by personal values, and it is the mixing of these two that determines whether a person is of "good character" or "bad character." For example, a person may have a high degree of perseverance and thus be capable of sustained effort toward the achievement of chosen objectives. If this person's values are weak or misguided, however, he may persevere toward undesirable or illegal ends. For example, many of the Spanish conquistadors of the sixteenth century had a remarkable degree of perseverance. Perseverance sustained them over long and arduous voyages and on dangerous marches through the swamps and forests of the New World. For many of these adventurers, however, values that placed gold and silver above human life resulted in looting and the destruction of indigenous populations. Character, then, must be tempered by higher values.

Character and values were seldom discussed in the business environment of the 1980s—except in the negative. This is changing. Rich Teerlink, CEO of Harley Davidson notes, "I find that when I go out and talk with people, the issue of character and values comes up, people are talking about it more. I think it's a recognition that it really is the best way to operate a business in the long run and that it's in everybody's best interest."

Business leaders of the 1990s are more than ever interested in the character of the people who work for them, and in their personal ethical standards. An executive must have, according to Paul N. Howell, Chairman and CEO of Howell Corporation, "the willingness and demonstrated ability to conduct him- or herself on a high moral and ethical level in both business and personal life. Without it, success is uncertain and short lived." Jack Bogle speaks strongly about character:

> It means integrity; it means other people can trust you which is a variation of that; it means you don't have a hidden agenda; that you're straightforward and when you say something you mean it; that you can be believed. Imagine trying to run a company if people didn't believe you. Just imagine. The more I see of business the more I think people really like to be associated with a highly ethical firm. I think it makes a big difference to people. I believe that the character of the company, and I guess one just has to take for granted that the character of the leader is reflected in the character of the company, is extremely important in running an organization . . .

The idea that "greed is good," as spoken by the takeover tycoon in the movie *Wall Street,* is viewed as an aberration of the last decade, and one that would have a very small following in the world of commerce today. The abuses associated with hostile takeovers—dishonesty, lack of integrity, and illegal practices in the financial markets—tried the tolerance of citizens, regulators and many managers, leading to a backlash. Employees, customers, and shareholders alike suffered the excesses and avarice of a few people who betrayed the trust and responsibility of their positions.

The events of the past decade notwithstanding, business has always had image problems—most often stemming from the lack of character or integrity on the part of prominent executives. Ever since the beginning of the Industrial Age, business leaders have been variously admired and hated—loved for their great inventiveness and philanthropy, and hated for their immense wealth and misanthropy. Thomas Edison, inventor and founding genius of General Electric, was universally admired for the way his new inventions changed the lives of ordinary people; John D. Rockefeller, on the other hand, became "the most hated man in America." Others, notably J.P. Morgan, were both admired and feared for the great power they held over the purse strings of corporate America.

Today, public attitudes toward business are formed around the actions of corporate leaders with respect to employment in our inner cities, the environment, and in the treatment of long-term employees caught between the pincers of downsizing and technological change. Corporations must recognize the existence of broader constituencies. Shareholders are no longer the only faction that must be served: there are unions, communities, employees and environmental values.

Present economic conditions no longer support the kind of wanton self-serving that has given business a bad name through the decades. Business leaders now know what the best in their trade have always understood—that the managers and executives who are lacking in the attributes of character that earn them the respect and trust of their subordinates don't last long in the corporation of the 1990s.

Character is the decision maker's compass. Scholars who have studied the nature of managerial work generally describe it in these terms:

- The manager's day is a series of interruptions.
- The manager's attention shifts rapidly from one issue to another.
- Decisions are required in an environment of uncertainty and ambiguity.
- Managers have little time for planning and systematic thinking.

In other words, managerial life is turbulent, fast changing, and highly ambiguous. Given this description, executives need something that is solid, unchanging, and certain from which to chart their course. Character and the virtues that go with it (honesty, integrity, etc.) provide that solid base for the decision maker. They are a moral compass that the executive can always refer to in getting his or her bearings. Dean Keller confirmed this when he said:

> Strong values and ethics are timeless and provide the guideposts we need to grow and flourish in a complex, changing world. Ultimately, executive success—yesterday, today or tomorrow—comes from within. It must be related to having a strong personal anchor and a strong, rigorously developed sense of values and ethics.

One of the best examples of character in action is found in the case of Jim Burke, then CEO of Johnson & Johnson, and his handling of the Tylenol™ poisoning tragedy. Burke made the decision to pull Tylenol capsules off the market. His sense of what was right along with a guiding set of corporate values rallied his staff to handle the situation in a manner that showed accountability to both consumers and shareholders. Jim Burke recalls dealing with the crisis:

> If you look at the Tylenol situation, the reason that the country was so responsive was not really me, it was because the company I represented had a hundred years of relationships with the public and had built a sense of trust. What they were doing by trusting demonstrated that they believed in the character of Johnson & Johnson, a character that had been epitomized by all of its leadership. But beyond that it was very central to the

company to be concerned about all of their constituencies and to recognize, through a document we all live by called the "Credo," that those constituencies are interrelated and that we are in business to serve society, and if you did that well you ended up making more money for your stockholders over the long run.

The idea of the "credo" (see Figure 3–1) has become extremely important in the last decade, as businesses strive to create a particular corporate culture and foster character values across the company. The Johnson & Johnson Credo talks about responsibility, the responsibility of the corporation to its primary consumers, to its employees, to its host communities, and to its stockholders. The proliferation of corporate "credos" speaks to the prevalence of the concern of corporate leaders with ethical issues, accountability, and standards that are meant to guide company decision makers in times of crises, such as the Tylenol incident.

The Credo and the management of Jim Burke and his successor Ralph Larsen have made Johnson & Johnson the most studied corporation in the world and an example of forging a corporate culture out of a strong commitment to ethical practices.

Senior Executives Talk about Character

It is the sine qua non of building trust, mutual concern and individual owning-up to responsibility among constituents. (Shirley D. Brinsfield, chairman and president, Curtiss-Wright Corp., Lyndhurst, NJ.)

Executive success cannot be achieved without earning and maintaining the respect and confidence of one's associates through displaying the common traits of high character—such traits as integrity, consistency, dependability, etc. (George Wackenhut, chairman and CEO, The Wackenhut Corp., Coral Gables, FL.)

Character is a combination of demonstrated personal traits and convictions—including ethics, candor, and fairness—that earn the respect of others. What a person does, not just what a person says. An executive lacking character may achieve success in the short term, but fails eventually by mistrust among those whose contributions are essential to his or her success. (Douglas C.

Our Credo

We believe our first responsibility is to the doctors, nurses and patients,
to mothers and fathers and all others who use our products and services.
In meeting their needs everything we do must be of high quality.
We must constantly strive to reduce our costs
in order to maintain reasonable prices.
Customers' orders must be serviced promptly and accurately.
Our suppliers and distributors must have an opportunity
to make a fair profit.

We are responsible to our employees,
the men and women who work with us throughout the world.
Everyone must be considered as an individual.
We must respect their dignity and recognize their merit.
They must have a sense of security in their jobs.
Compensation must be fair and adequate,
and working conditions clean, orderly and safe.
We must be mindful of ways to help our employees fulfill
their family responsibilities.
Employees must feel free to make suggestions and complaints.
There must be equal opportunity for employment, development
and advancement for those qualified.
We must provide competent management,
and their actions must be just and ethical.

We are responsible to the communities in which we live and work
and to the world community as well.
We must be good citizens — support good works and charities
and bear our fair share of taxes.
We must encourage civic improvements and better health and education.
We must maintain in good order
the property we are privileged to use,
protecting the environment and natural resources.

Our final responsibility is to our stockholders.
Business must make a sound profit.
We must experiment with new ideas.
Research must be carried on, innovative programs developed
and mistakes paid for.
New equipment must be purchased, new facilities provided
and new products launched.
Reserves must be created to provide for adverse times.
When we operate according to these principles,
the stockholders should realize a fair return.

Johnson & Johnson

Figure 3–1   The Johnson & Johnson Credo

Yearley, chairman, president, and CEO, Phelps Dodge Corp., Phoenix, AZ.)

It's the key reason for success. (Craig Benson, chairman and COO, Cabletown Systems Inc., Rochester, NH.)

Developing Character

In character development, steadfastness and resoluteness become necessary to make difficult, sometimes unpopular decisions. In this day, mavericks are needed to push business beyond its limits. One cannot be a maverick without a strong belief in oneself. This belief and self-assurance develop out of experience, out of making tough decisions, dealing with the consequences and learning from mistakes.

Experience is the best teacher in matters of character. Parents, teachers, workplace mentors, and the like can demonstrate the attributes of fine character, but, usually, these cannot be internalized without some real life experiences. In other words, those aspiring to succeed in business have to go out and do—become involved, take action, take risks (not foolish ones), and stretch their personal sphere.

Success requires the capacity to learn. One of the emerging trends in business is that ambitious people do much more volunteering than their counterparts. They step forward to take on new projects, work on problems, or take assignments that move them into an entirely different venue for a period of time. They are willing to step out of their comfort zone and take a risk on themselves. If you are afraid to make mistakes, you won't push the envelope as far as it can be pushed; you won't accomplish what could have been accomplished.

There is truth, also, in the popular wisdom that says adversity builds character. Only by sticking one's neck out a little can a person meet challenges that test his or her abilities and provide the opportunity to surpass limitations. Failure is not the issue. In fact, failure can provide valuable learning experiences. The key, in terms of long term career success, is what you have learned from your failures and mistakes. These experiences can add depth to your knowledge and understanding. "That's why I'm interested in people who have failed," notes Paul Austermuehle, President of TMP Worldwide. It is important that, in the course of a career, you show that you can take responsibility for mistakes and failures, learn from them, and move on. Surprisingly, the number of people willing to take responsibility for mistakes and failure is small. Those who do surely stand out in a positive light.

Seasoned executives give these recommendations to aspiring executives who are interested in developing character:

> Character is developed through a sense of stewardship developed by encouraging senior managers to view themselves as surrogates for the firm's constituents. Be prepared to endure the pain of being expected to do the right thing in the right way under conditions of high uncertainty. (S. D. Brinsfield, chairman and president, Curtiss-Wright Corp., Lyndhurst, NJ.)

> Character is developed through the mentoring of senior leaders who are leading by good example. Be honest, be candid, respect the individual, let your actions speak louder than words. (David S. Boyer, president, Teleflex Inc., Plymouth Meeting, PA.)

> The fundamentals of character are developed through family and community associations long before an individual joins a business. The senior executive can enhance the character of associates by example, by mentoring and by molding the corporate culture to encourage ethics, candor and fairness. Always be fair and ethical. If you betray your character, you suffer a loss within yourself and within the organization that may never be regained. (Douglas C. Yearley, chairman, president, and CEO, Phelps Dodge Corporation., Phoenix, AZ.)

> It cannot be taught. It can be fostered in a company, but the basic ingredient must be inside the individual. You must give a damn about your company, it's success and the customers. (Craig Benson, chairman, COO, Cabletown Systems Inc., Rochester, NH.)

> Character is developed through experience on the job; a well rounded, diverse life outside of work. Don't shirk opportunities to address tough issues; volunteer and pitch in! (Roger A. Young, president, Bay State Gas Co., Westborough, MA.)

LEADERSHIP

Americans have a penchant for certain types of things—loud music, barbecues, endless variety, and a ceaseless quest for

the perfect leader. In recent years, the voting public has
sought great leaders and learned to live with disappointment.
In the business world, the decline of the great icons of American industry—GM, IBM, Sears, Digital Equipment, Eastern Air-
lines, and dozens of others—suggests that the finger of
blame—typically pointed at ordinary workers—should actually be pointed at top managers and the directors that engage
them. Richard Leucke complains that "in our bones we have a
sense that our progress is in the hands of managers and ten-
ders of the organizational machinery, not true leaders: people
who know how to keep the trains running on schedule, but
who cannot see beyond where the tracks are already laid. We
will make no progress without the leaders and the seers who
can extend the tracks in new directions, we will merely travel
around on the same route."[1]

And we do seek them. Over the past few decades, almost
3,000 books and articles have been written on leadership.
Seminars and workshops on the subject enjoy capacity en-
rollments. We admire leaders, and hope to emulate them. We
are continually seeking to unlock the secrets of effective
leadership.

Great leaders throughout history have used a number of
styles: personal bravery (Alexander the Great), fear (Attila),
eloquence (Churchill), charisma (T.E. Lawrence), coalition
building (Franklin Roosevelt), autocracy (Patton), and ideas
(Martin Luther).

The late General George Patton is among the most successful and admired leaders, and is considered one of the most effective military leaders in America's history. What may be
most significant about Patton, for our purposes, is that he
became a great leader through a matter of will and effort. He
transformed himself from a soft-spoken, mild-mannered person, into the fiery dynamo whose name became legend among
his troops and his opponents. While he may have lacked a winning personality, there is no denying his effectiveness as a military leader.

Leaders may be born, but Patton showed that leaders can
also be made. Indeed, methods developed by the armed forces
and many businesses are premised on the idea that even those

not blessed with natural leadership can develop the qualities that make it possible to influence and lead others.

Changing Styles of Leadership

Leadership in business used to follow Patton's autocratic style. It meant getting people to do what you wanted them to do, plain and simple. It was based upon the complementary dyad of one person giving orders and others following them. Autocratic leaders are stern, tough, and unyielding. They view any difference of opinion as a challenge to their authority. These leaders spend much of their energy maintaining the boundaries of this fragile authority. Disagreements, differences of opinion, divergences from the rules, and certainly any indication of actual conflict are seen as threats to control and stability.

In the military, this may indeed be the best model of leadership. And at a certain point in American business history, there may have been good reason to exercise this kind of leadership style. It is the model associated with the bureaucratic, hierarchical organization.

Today, shifting trends in business and among the work force are redefining the role of the leader. That role is changing from the old autocratic model based on fear to one proposed 2,500 years ago by Lao Tzu: "To lead the people, walk behind them." Today, motivating factors other than fear must be taken into consideration. People's need for competency, for recognition, for meaning and dignity have become overriding considerations. People today have an enlarged capacity to be self-motivated. It is up to business leaders to develop and nurture this capacity for self-direction, creativity, and talent in their work force. This model of leadership depends less on direction from the top than on providing a vision for others to follow, and on inspiring others to do their best in the pursuit of that vision. It is a leadership model that is more in keeping with non-hierarchical organizations of today than with the command and control organizations of the past.

Ray Stata, Chairman and President of Analog Devices noted this need to shift leadership styles when he said:

Historically, leaders were referred to as "captain of the ship" to denote their role in operating the vessel entrusted to their care. Future leaders must be both designers and operators. Their principal contribution will be to shape the design of the organizational structure and policies so as to best fulfill the corporate mission.

Complementing Stata's views on modern leadership is the work of Michael Maccoby who, in his study of leadership traits and development, identified three qualities that all competent leaders share: "a caring, respectful, and responsible attitude; flexibility about people and organizational structure; and a participative approach to management, the willingness to share power."[2] These are qualities that will carry you through the challenges of the contemporary workplace. Leaders of the present and future must operate in a culture of openness, tolerance, creativity, and productivity—an environment in which people are treated humanely, and are able to bring out their best. In doing so, they can follow Lao Tzu's timeless advice:

> The best of all leaders is the one who helps people so that, eventually, they don't need him. . . .
>
> The best leader doesn't say much, but what he says carries weight.
>
> When he is finished with his work, the people say, "It happened naturally."

John Kotter addressed another facet of this issue in his notable book, *A Force for Change: How Management Differs From Leadership.*[3] His more recent work expands:

> Between 1930 and 1970 "many firms performed very well with managers and executives spending much more time managing than leading. With demand equal to or greater than supply in many industries, the key to success was simply getting the product out the door on time and on budget. In a more competitive and changing . . . environment, this is no longer true. In some industries, supply exceeds demand. In others, what is being bought is constantly changing. In both cases, it is no longer effective to do well only what has been done in the past.

To succeed, organizations now need to reduce costs, improve quality, develop new products, and move much faster. The capacity to produce useful change is becoming more and more the key to success. And change requires leadership."

In the late 1980s Kotter interviewed the ten top executives in each of twenty business firms that had all been very economically successful over the previous five to ten years. "Outstanding leaders were described as people who made sure an organization had clear and sensible direction, usually by helping to create a vision of the future and strategies for achieving that vision. Leaders were said to communicate that direction widely and in such a way as to get relevant parties to both understand it and believe it is appropriate. Great leaders were also described as being unusually good at motivating or inspiring people so that when progress toward a vision encountered serious problems there was enough energy to break through the barriers. In doing all this, leaders were said to produce change—developing new organizations or businesses and helping old ones to adapt to a shifting business environment."

"In this new economic environment and in network-like organizational forms, executives who cannot lead are increasingly having problems. If they are surrounded by other non-leaders, their firms usually perform poorly unless protected in some way. If they are surrounded by leaders, people who cannot lead are increasingly being passed over for promotion. This pattern can be easily seen within Harvard's Class of '74. Those individuals who manage but do not lead are in lower-level positions, are making less money, and are in slower-growing businesses than their classmates."

This prompts Kotter's New Rule #5: "Success in managerial jobs increasingly requires leadership, not just good management. Even at lower levels in firms, the inability to lead is hurting both corporate performance and individual careers. Organizations that stifle leadership from employees are no longer winning."[4]

Hedrick Smith quotes Bellcore CEO George Heilmeier on changes in the relationship between management and leadership. "[T]he Harvard Business School tells you, by golly, if you get an MBA from Harvard Business School, you can manage anything. But this is more than management—it's leadership, and Harvard Business School doesn't teach you anything about leadership. Management is all about running an enterprise in a smooth manner. Leadership's all about change. Now, you might say, 'Well what do we need in this country, management or leadership?' It's not either/or, you need both. Unfortunately, in this country we've tended to swing the pendulum too far to the management side."[5]

Executives in our survey also noted how the nature of leadership is changing:

> Leaders are becoming more like coaches than directors. (Dan Bollom, president and CEO, Wisconsin Public Service Corp., Green Bay, WI.)

> Autocratic leaders are no longer in vogue and the younger generation is not receptive to either bureaucracy or wishy-washy leadership. (David S. Boyer, president, Teleflex Inc., Plymouth Meeting, PA.)

> The emergence of the flat organization—fewer layers of management separating senior managers from the operating levels—increases the importance of leadership at all levels. (Douglas C. Yearley, chairman, president, and CEO, Phelps Dodge Corp., Phoenix, AZ.)

> The majority want to be led into battle—lead them. Others want to lead—give them opportunity to do so. When others show the ability to lead, leaders must become support people, encouraging that ability, providing opportunities for its development. It's a different kind of strength than that exhibited by traditional autocratic leaders. (Frank Evans, regional director of recruiting for Deloitte & Touche, Cincinnati, OH.)

> Leadership is getting people to strive for and to accomplish the vision. This includes the motivational aspects of wanting to do it. To me, if you can't do that, you're not an executive. That's what the person is being paid to do. It's not the number crunching but it's getting people together. If you don't accomplish the vision, then you've not achieved anything. (Mark Spool, director of Organizational Development and Executive Development for ARCO Chemical, Newtown Square, PA.)

Developing Leadership Skills

Those seeking executive positions must develop leadership skills. Companies want people who can take charge, who can provide direction and get the most out of others. Based upon our executive survey, executives should develop the ability to:

- Create a vision that others can follow.
- Gain the willful cooperation of others.
- Focus and motivate the organization in strategic directions.
- Influence change in an organization.
- Think strategically.
- Listen, communicate, and relate to others in a meaningful way.
 - Tolerate and accept criticism to engender constructive conflict and differences.
- Ask questions, receive advice and opinions, not just give orders.

VISION

Vision is an element of competent leadership, yet is worthy of discussion as a separate issue. Vision separates highly successful people from their counterparts. While the ethics and values of good character are the foundation of a successful career, and the ability to move and motivate people is the hallmark of leadership, vision provides the direction, the stimulus or reason for movement.

Vision is the ability to see beyond the present, to imagine what could be. It is out of this ability to imagine the possible that new things can be created, or be brought about. As recently retired Johnson & Johnson Vice Chairman Bob Campbell comments: "Vision is something that frequently will set apart the more successful executive. You're looking beyond those things that you're currently involved in, always recognizing the fact that there has to be constant renewal if you're going to stay ahead."

Vision for the business executive is not revelatory or magical. It is practical and grounded in reality. It involves risks, because the future always holds uncertainty, but taking risks is one of the things that sets successful executives apart.

Former Chrysler Chairman Lee Iacocca is often cited as an executive who had both vision and the skill and courage to pursue it. Harvard management professor John Kotter has written:

> Iacocca developed an agenda for himself and the firm that included a bold new vision of what Chrysler could and should be. It was a vision of a competitive and profitable firm that produced much higher quality products, provided better employment opportunities, and was strong enough to survive in the increasingly competitive automobile industry. It was a vision that valued all the important groups with a stake in the business. . . .[6]

Iacocca's vision, by itself, would have been sterile but for the fact he made it the basis for an intelligent and workable strategy around which he could rally Chrysler workers, lenders, and suppliers. It was this ability to connect vision with practical planning and action that saved Chrysler from economic collapse and made its chairman a national icon. As a new or mid-level manager, you will not be expected to create a vision of the magnitude produced by Iacocca. Nevertheless, the ability to envision where your department or your company might be at some given point in the future, the understanding of how it is situated in the larger economic environment, to be able to set goals and attain them—these are the hard currency of executive capability that your employer will be looking for. Vision of this sort requires real knowledge and understanding of the global economy, and of your own business and industry. It requires real skills in shaping and molding the organization so that it is in position to meet the goals you've set for it. It is the vision that gives the company a future. As Jack Bogle puts it:

Any successful executive is going to have to size up the world that lies beyond his view. There's a guy here that calls it "seeing around the corner," "seeing beyond the horizon," whatever you want to do. The ship is actually a great example. If you're going to sail that ship across the Atlantic Ocean, you're going to want to know every little thing that is out there ahead of you that can't really be predicted except by common sense and judgement. This is not a great skill, but it is an unusual one. It often requires the most painful of all things—thinking.

Additionally, Jack Bogle describes vision for the extraordinary Vanguard Group of Investment Companies in this way:

Vision . . . is looking out, trying to size up the environment . . . in terms of trying to figure out what logical things there are for people to do and buy and ways to invest.

Bogle is talking about being able to assess, where possible, those circumstances that affect one's business within some range of predictability and using those insights to direct corporate plans and actions. This has less to do with crystal ball gazing than listening to the marketplace in the broadest sense and applying knowledge and know-how. It's asking the right questions of the right people and being perceptive enough to hear the answers.

Senior Executives Talk about Vision

Vision is what you want to become. Everyone must know where you want the organization to go or you will never get there. (Dan Bollom, president and CEO, Wisconsin Public Service, Green Bay, WI.)

Vision is the ability to articulate where one wants to position the company in the future. It's essential to defining a strategic direction/plan and subsequent tactical actions. It's having the ability and desire to execute for the long term. (Roger A. Young, president, Bay State Gas Co., Westborough, MA.)

Vision is the ability to recognize the significance of current indicators of future events or trends. All business enterprises must be future-oriented. Those that possess it are always on the leading edge of new developments and are consistently innovative in their approach to business opportunities. (George R. Wackenhut, chairman and CEO, The Wackenhut Corp., Coral Gables, FL.)

Vision is a first cousin to change. Where is the successful executive who hasn't learned to cope with change? (Paul N. Howell, chairman, CEO, Howell Corp., Houston, TX.)

Vision is the ability to rise above today's mess and see what others are blind to. Without vision an organization can't anticipate and slowly fades. (Doug Rock, Smith International, Inc., Houston, TX.)

Those corporations that are unable to articulate a vision have difficulty competing in their markets. (David S. Boyer, president, Teleflex, Inc., Plymouth Meeting, PA.)

Vision is the ability to develop a mental image of the way an organization would function if it is to be successful. Without it, you cannot be a senior executive. (R. B. Williams, senior vice president, Enserch Corp/LoneStar Gas Co., Dallas, TX.)

Ultimately, what matters is being able to transfer that vision to others—the people whose job it is to make it happen, individuals on the shop floor or in the front lines of service. Unless executives can share their vision effectively throughout the organization, they will meet with limited success in achieving their goals. This translation of vision into the attainment of business goals will be addressed by the remaining three elements of success. These elements—quality, productivity, and functional expertise—are concerned with the aspect of success that separates those who ultimately succeed from those who fail—that is, the ability to get things done and to demonstrate it through measurable achievements.

QUALITY

Until twenty years ago, most American executives looked at quality in a very narrow sense: as either a measure of a physical product's conformance to design specifications or what Joseph Juran described as "fitness for use." These definitions were associated with statistical quality control methods developed at AT&T's Western Electric division during the 1930s. Executives viewed quality as a trade-off with cost. You either had high quality-high cost, or low quality-low cost.

The concept of quality expanded during the period of the 1950s through the 1980s. Missionaries of quality, like the late W. Edwards Deming and the scores of managers he educated in Japan and (later) in the United States, came to understand that quality was more than a simple statistical tool—it was an overarching philosophy for management that began with the customer and worked back through all the processes and activities of the enterprise and its suppliers. Deming developed a set of management principles that both expanded the concept of quality and challenged traditional ideas about managing. Among these principles were the following:

- Create constancy of purpose for improvement of product and service.
- Cease dependence on mass inspection to achieve quality.
- Improve constantly and forever the system of production and service.
- Drive out fear.
- Eliminate slogans, exhortations, and targets for the work force.
- Eliminate numerical quotas.
- Encourage education and self-improvement for everyone.[7]

By the late 1980s, AT&T expanded its own definition:

Quality is meeting customer expectations. The Quality Improvement Process is a set of principles, policies, support structures, and practices designed to continually improve the efficiency and effectiveness of our way of life.

Jack Bogle notes:

If you try to run a business without having a feeling for how you're doing with your client, you're a fool.

The new notion of quality—of quality as a way of doing business—extends to everything the company does. And it becomes management's job to support and improve it. As a result, executives are accountable for the quality of the entire range of activities that take place under their control. They have the ultimate responsibility for continual improvement in these activities and in meeting customer requirements. They must know how to define quality for their organizations, how to set realistic quality goals, and how to motivate others in achieving them.

Aspiring executives should understand that quality has a very personal dimension as well. In the age of Total Quality, they are judged according to the same exacting standards now being applied to product development, customers service, manufacturing, and other core processes through which companies serve markets. They are expected to produce quality output and to practice continuous improvement as individuals.

Progress toward a Total Quality ethos in U.S. business has been slow. According to quality consultant V. Daniel Hunt, American manufacturers still spend 20–25 percent of production costs in finding and correcting mistakes, compared with 3 percent in Japan.[8] (U.S. service industry companies are even worse, with an estimated 35 percent of operating costs dedicated to doing things wrong and doing them over.) And a decade after all the major quality management methodologies became known in North America, fewer than half of U.S. manufacturers have adopted quality programs.

Executives interviewed in our survey suggest that the commitment to quality must be considered a way of doing business, a way of being. Douglas Yearley, chairman and CEO of Phelps Dodge Corporation puts it this way: "Total Quality is a cultural blueprint for success. It's a process for integrating quality development, quality maintenance, and continuous quality improvement efforts. It is a commitment to excellence in which all organizational elements focus on the continuous process of improvement and conformance to requirements. Total quality is directly related to bottom line profits." Quality expert Philip Crosby confirmed Yearley's comment about profits when he wrote that half of the money *not* spent on correcting mistakes goes directly to the bottom line. In this sense, quality pays for itself in higher profits, which is what executives are expected to produce.

Senior Executives Talk about Quality

Quality is exceeding customers' expectations. You will not be successful over time without it. (Dan Bollom, president and CEO, Wisconsin Public Service, Green Bay, WI.)

No executive can expect to be considered if unable to consistently provide a quality product or service. (Paul N. Howell, chairman and CEO, Howell Corporation, Houston, TX.)

Quality is creating high expectations and exceeding them. This is how executives create value. ([Mr] Shirley D. Brinsfield, chairman and president, Curtiss-Wright Corp., Lyndhurst, NJ.)

Quality is meeting a customer's needs every time. (Doug Rock, chairman and CEO, Smith International, Inc., Houston, TX.)

At least a familiarity with the formal application of Total Quality programs is essential for a senior executive. (George Wackenhut, chairman and CEO, The Wackenhut Corp., Coral Gables, FL.)

Quality is meeting or surpassing the customer's specified needs in the area of product specifications, delivery, speed to market, product. Without superior quality no company can remain competitive today. It can be determined through customer audits and feedback, internal attitude toward quality and continuous improvement and internal focus on continuous improvement. (David S. Boyer, president, Teleflex Inc., Plymouth Meeting, PA.)

Quality performance can be attributed directly to an executive's commitment to excellence. (Ken Kollmeyer, senior vice-president Operations, Moore Medical Corp.)

Quality is a management process that marries efficiency and effectiveness with customer satisfaction. It provides a vital and valid tactical perspective in a competitive marketplace. (Roger A. Young, president, Bay State Gas Co.)

Quality is Customer-Oriented. Basically all of the modern quality management programs are customer-oriented. They begin with the customer—what he or she wants, the level of performance or service required—and work back through all of their processes. The best companies carry their obsession for quality back even further—into the supply chain; they require that their suppliers institute quality programs of their own. Many help suppliers in this effort and audit supplier quality programs.

Customers may be internal or external. Internal customers may be people in another department who require specific things from your department in order to get their jobs done. They may be in the same department. Your customers too may be those under you who require your expertise or guidance and leadership.

Executives must understand this customer-oriented quality and consistently act to support it.

PRODUCTIVITY

National radio icon Don Imus refers to it as "getting it done." More specifically, productivity is the ratio of outputs to inputs. Since most outputs and inputs can be measured, productivity itself can be measured. In today's environment of "do more faster with fewer resources," increased productivity is the key to success and the metric by which executives are being measured. Executives who can deliver greater output without having to beg for more workers and bigger budgets are sought out and promoted.

Productivity was less important in the less competitive environment of the early post-war years. Productivity, like career advancement, was driven by expanding markets. Everyone appeared productive because everything was getting bigger. Cost factors were less critical, resources less expensive, and waste hardly noticed. This is hardly the case today.

Productivity is tied to several critical areas, including the following:

• Cooperation of others.
• Management of processes.
• Appropriate use of technology.
• Effective time management.

While this is by no means a comprehensive list of the factors affecting overall productivity, nor even personal productivity, executives who can get these areas under control are able to raise productivity levels.

Cooperation of Others

Success is never solely the result of individual effort. It comes about through joint effort, and the most successful of such efforts is a result of the voluntary cooperation of others. Cooperation is a function of the respect and regard one has earned from colleagues and employees. Once these are earned, the task of leadership is greatly facilitated, gathering a momentum of its own and flowing from an energy source independent of any single person.

Management of Processes

The quality movement was instrumental in shifting management from its myopic focus on people to the process through which work was done. On the production floor, for example, managers traditionally cajoled people to work faster, and possibly gained a productivity increase of 5 percent. Following the principles of process improvement—for example, by redesigning work flows—these same managers could increase productivity by 50–70 percent in a single stroke.

Appropriate Use of Technology

Productivity is inextricably tied to technology. This has been the case since tools first came into use, since water power could be harnessed to do the work of a hundred men, and since computer controlled machines entered the modern factory. The executive must be educated about how technology can be used to increase productivity and how workers can be trained to make the most of it.

But technology is not in and of itself a sure bet for improving productivity. In the past, American industry has been overzealous in its belief that technology could close the quality and cost gaps between it and Japanese competitors. General Motors, for example, invested billions in technology—primarily computer controlled production equipment; IBM invested heavily in computers for clerical operations. Neither of these initiatives paid off as intended because, according to critics, they simply tried to do with machines what people were doing by hand. The processes to which the technology was applied had not been redesigned. By comparison, Japanese companies generally lag behind U.S. firms in the application of technology to work, yet their annual rate of productivity increases is higher because their people-driven processes are better designed. As Dan Bollom has stated, "Productivity gets better by continuous improvement of the processes."

Effective Time Management

Time management is a science unto itself, and a great deal of research is available on the topic. Executives have always had tremendous demands on their time and these have only increased as organizations have gotten flatter. Time, however, is a resource that cannot be expanded. Therefore, it is imperative that we make the most of it through time-use habits that increase productivity. Managing one's time begins with setting goals and prioritizing them on a daily, weekly, and monthly basis. Goals are important for obvious reasons. They are, in effect, the raison d'être for a period of time. But some goals are more important than others in terms of their results for the company, and this fact must be considered when allocating the available amount of time among goals. R.C. Dorney, a time management expert, advises executives to observe Pareto's Law—that 80 percent of the outcomes are a result of 20 percent of activities.[9] The implication here is that you need to identify the handful of goals that contain the greatest payoff for the company, then allocate the lion's share of your time to these. Less important goals can either be deferred or delegated to others.

Charles R. Hobbs, president of a management consulting corporation and developer of the Time Power Seminar, advises, "Schedule a few minutes at the beginning of each week to write and prioritize weekly goals. Schedule a few minutes each day to organize the day's activities. In each of the planning periods, list everything you have to do during the week or day."

EXPERTISE

Writing in *Fortune* magazine on managerial careers, Walter Kiechel III advises that "from your very first day on the job, you have to bring something, some special expertise, to the party." Kiechel cites an Intel executive as telling new recruits that, "Even as a manager, you have to add value. You have to be good at something in the arena you're working in. You can't just say, 'Well, I am a manager so I will just manage and coordinate these people.' People don't require that kind of management any more."[10] From the first week on the job, you must demonstrate an identifiable skill.

Expertise is defined as current, usable knowledge. The type of expertise you will need changes as you grow in your career. In the early stages, expertise usually refers to the mastery of some technical or functional area, such as accounting, financial analysis, market research, or information systems. It is expertise that makes it possible for managers to make frontline decisions with confidence. The recognition of this expertise by co-workers and subordinates leads to their support of those decisions and directions.

In her book *Becoming A Manager,* Harvard professor Linda Hill quotes a sales manager, who describes how expertise from ten years as a salesperson has made him more effective as a manager:

> It gives me credibility with the reps. They say, "He has experience with both the up and down swings of the economy" versus "How can this guy tell me what to do?" They know I've probably seen it before. When they come for advice they feel they can trust me. . . . There is no [technical] problem that is going to come up that I don't know how to grab onto and do something about.[11]

The point is, everyone must bring something to the organization, something tangible.

Expertise and the Executive Career

Business scholars have observed that technical expertise is more important in the earlier stages of an executive career than in later, senior-management stages. During these early stages, executives are more intimately involved in the details of functional activities, often at a hands-on level. Decision making is limited to local issues, often of a technical nature. There is not a lot of demand for strategic vision from lower-level executives.

As the executive progresses in his or her career, however, decision making becomes more strategic and visionary and less focused on issues requiring specific technical or functional expertise. The technical details become the concern of staff functionaries. People and organizational issues grow in importance. These are issues that require a different kind of knowledge than that required by a specific functional or technical area. Good business judgment becomes more important than specific technical expertise. Figure 3–2 illustrates the executive's evolving requirements for expertise.

As the figure makes clear, technical issues—the kind that require expertise in making effective functional decisions—become less and less important as a manager or executive moves to higher levels. In other words, as the executive's career

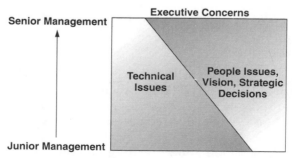

Figure 3–2 Technical Expertise and the Executive

advances, he or she must become more of a generalist in knowledge and outlook. As stated before, your functional expertise gives you credibility in the long run and nitty-gritty experience from which to extrapolate. The specific knowledge gained by mastering a functional area becomes the jumping off point for attaining a broader outlook and knowledge base. Knowledge of processes, cycles in your particular industry, and sensitivity to trends and what they may portend are required of the upper level executive.

Jack Bogle emphasizes the need for experiences before being able to lead a company:

> Absolutely essential—a lifetime of experience in a given business is, in the long run, almost the only way you can run that business or at least run it to its optimum extent. I'm a very hands-on person, a very detailed person, I've been in this business a long time and I know it well. I couldn't do my job without knowing it, and I really basically don't think I could do it unless I know more than the next guy.

Obviously, broadening your experience and knowledge-base does not occur over night. Thoughtful preparation—a career plan that includes expanding your understanding and knowledge—is key. If you haven't done that, then on the day you step out from the secure world of your functional expertise into the world of upper level decision making, you are likely to fall flat on your face.

Continuous Learning

One way to avoid such a fall is to develop early in your career an ethic of continuous learning. The closed mind is the fastest road to obsolescence. In fact, executives have said that the number one reason for failure of new executives is they are not prepared for the job at hand. They don't know what they need to know in order to succeed because during their early careers they did not keep learning.

The zest for continuous learning is a trait shared by all successful individuals. They know that change undermines the value of their training and education over time and they understand that the world is larger, more complex, and more interconnected than anything they were prepared to expect. The accelerated rate of change that is part and parcel of the information age breeds obsolescence. And the complexities of a globalized marketplace require constant vigilance of business trends all over the world.

Successful individuals are not content to rest on their current knowledge but pursue new knowledge in a systematic way. As a junior executive, you'll want to be one of these individuals. As a senior executive, you'll want to identify and retain as many of them as possible as employees.

There are, however, two approaches to continuous learning and the differences between them lead to different career outcomes. Eric Sevareid once remarked in a dinner speech that "we are discovering that we have two types of people: those who know more and more about less and less—the 'specialists'—and those who know less and less about more and more—the 'generalists.' If this continues, we'll soon have a world in which one group knows everything about nothing, while the other group understands nothing about everything."

Sevareid's warning about the extremes of these two approaches to learning notwithstanding, it is clear from the discussion in Chapter 1 that the future work place will have a growing number of highly educated specialists, "knowledgeable workers" as Drucker calls them, for whom the details of their fields will be mastered as a "craft." Here we think of computer systems specialists, financial analysts, research scientists, safety managers, and so forth. Many readers, even holders of MBA degrees, will be numbered among these professionals and technical specialists. They have every reason to learn "more and more about less and less," both to keep current with changes in their fields, and to master the growing complexity of their work.

There will be another, smaller group that will represent the core management of the corporation. Although most will have started their careers in a specific functional or technical area, this group is challenged to both keep up with some of the technical changes in their functions, so that they can make informed decisions, and to broaden their understanding of global events, changes in their industry, and the connectedness between their markets, competitors, and the many parts of their businesses. They have a need for broader understandings, particularly at the level of senior management. However, even at junior levels, these professionals must know enough about the different functional areas to be able to properly coordinate them.

Just as the general manager cannot sacrifice technical expertise entirely in pursuit of the big picture, a technical professional should not ignore wider issues and trends in the business community in general. There is a great need for good "business" people in all functions and levels, and this may be what Sevareid anticipated: that professionals need to have a well-rounded education and perspective.

Technology

One particular area of concern for the nontechnical executive is technology and its management. Technology is changing so fast that the core competencies upon which a company's products are based can become obsolete very quickly. We need look no further than the computer industry for evidence of this; there, technological change has made it possible for high-powered, low cost work stations to undermine traditional mainframe computing. This example is repeated yearly in countless industries and markets as innovation creates turmoil and progress. To stay in business, executives must peer into the future and recognize the technological capabilities their companies will need to survive and lead. They must then build or buy those capabilities. This is easier said than done, since it is rarely clear which of several competing technologies will come to dominate a market. Executives at RCA faced this problem in the late 1970s when they chose videodisc technology over competing VHS and BETA technologies. In retrospect we know that theirs was the wrong choice, and it led to an enormously costly failure for RCA. At the time the decision was made, however, the future looked much different.

For the non-technical executive in particular, keeping abreast of new technology and allocating resources for competing R&D projects is a daunting problem for which there are no universal solutions. To make good decisions with respect to technology, executives need to know the technology, their markets, and their business operations. This requires both continuous learning about technologies and an understanding that the future will not be a simple repetition of the past.

The Global View

Expertise is also required in the area of global business. The globalization of markets and increased international competition have created the need for a more worldly executive who is cross-culturally aware, able to understand the impact of world economies on local economies. Not only is there a wide range of foreign-owned companies in the United States but American companies have interests spanning the globe. The executive that makes a point of becoming multiculturally educated will be better positioned to contribute to a multinational company.

The international community is restructuring along predominantly economic lines. Political ideology is taking a back seat to economics as nations jockey for favorable positions in an increasingly linked, interdependent world economy. The interdependence of markets means that the effects of a worker strike or revolution halfway across the globe will likely have an impact on your business. Conversely, a policy-decision you make in your office at headquarters may well reverberate to the shop floor of workers who speak a language you may have never heard of. You will need to have a pretty good idea of what the effects of both scenarios are likely to be. Cross-cultural sensitivity, knowledge of political and economic issues that link the globe, understanding of the difficulties of developing economies, and the ability to maneuver in the sometimes narrow spaces created by struggling governments and rapidly changing economic structures are among the skills you will want to develop.

Taking foreign assignments is an important way to gain on-the-ground experience, and these kinds of cross-cultural experiences are becoming more and more valued in executive circles.

Learning from foreign assignments and from the practices of other cultures can add tremendous depth and breadth to an executive's repertoire of management skills. "What is needed is an in-depth understanding and appreciation of at least one other culture which can be extrapolated to other cultures, languages, and scenarios," says James J. Beirne, graduate career development and placement director of the Wharton School.

Talking with colleagues who have worked in other countries, maintaining links with foreign colleagues and reading widely are additional ways to add depth and breadth to your repertoire of management skills and to build your foundation of knowledge and understanding.

SUMMARY

The role of the executive is a dynamic one. The elements addressed in this chapter provide a good base from which to direct and build an executive career. As the key elements identified by successful executives, they can be viewed as a starting part for developing your career, for strengthening it, and for positioning yourself for the future.

In the next chapter we give you some pointers on career management. Again, we draw on our data base of executives to provide suggestions for practical ways to manage your career.

4

MANAGING A SUCCESSFUL CAREER

*The individual has to take more responsibility for himself
or herself, rather than depend on the company.*

Peter F. Drucker

The factors which forced the changes that began in the early 1980s still remain and, by all indications, will continue well into the future. Unlike the business downturns of a previous era, the present period is more than just another business cycle. Not everything is going to go back to the way it was.

The resulting changes are here to stay. Unfortunately, the changes in corporate structure and priorities have run head-on into the long-standing tradition in the American workplace of providing good employees with job security and upward mobility. As Rosabeth Kantor put it, "The job-tenure ideal is colliding with the job-insecurity reality."[1] Suddenly, long term employees have found themselves displaced.

The manner in which "redundant" workers are handled varies widely from company to company. The best companies provide career counseling and placement assistance.

70

After consolidating several of its operating units in the late 1980s, Johnson & Johnson offered career assistance services with the objective of helping affected personnel find other positions within Johnson & Johnson or, failing that, to find employment elsewhere. During the first group session a 20 year employee began to weep while clutching a copy of the Johnson & Johnson "Credo." The Credo, which is viewed as the ultimate authority within Johnson & Johnson, does not guarantee employment, but does spell out the corporation's commitment to the well-being of each employee.

The despondent employee was clearly concerned that the corporation's faithfulness might be falling short of the Credo's spirit in some important way. For years, there had been an unspoken and unwritten belief within the company that people who worked hard and did their jobs well would have cradle-to-grave employment. But this was now changing.[2] In response, Johnson & Johnson formally established a Corporate Career Center. The Center was designed to provide comprehensive job search assistance to displaced employees and is now the most effective organization of its kind in the country.

The crying employee with Credo in hand was soon thereafter rehired by another Johnson & Johnson operating unit. But not everyone affected by corporate reorganization can be so fortunate.

What continues to happen across America is a conflict between the corporation's need to remain fiscally strong and operationally competitive, and the employee's need for meaningful, long term work. As we have discussed in previous chapters, conflict has been working to the disadvantage of many long term employees. The new realities call for different assumptions and different strategies.

In the new world of work, thoughtful corporations are moving away from the notion of lifetime employment to the broader notion of "employability." These firms offer the employee something quite different than the expectation of a permanent position: they offer challenging work and an opportunity to learn, grow, develop and hone marketable skills. It becomes the responsibility of the employee to make the most of these. In effect, these corporations are requiring employees to take charge of their own career development—to become owners of their own "businesses."

EXECUTIVE AS BUSINESS PROPRIETOR

Executives and newly-minted M.B.A.'s know what it takes to run a business. They can tell you without hesitation what a successful business must have:

- A valued product or service to sell at a competitive price.
- Planning.
- Research and development.
- Well-tuned operations.
- Information systems.
- Sales and customer service.
- Public relations.
- Administration.
- Financing.

Creating and managing these essential business activities is what executives are trained to do; it's what they are hired and paid for. Ironically, many of these same people do not recognize that they must see their own careers in the same light. They fail to see that progress in their own careers is ultimately a function of acquiring and engaging the same business capabilities. They fail to see themselves as CEOs of their own businesses—businesses that must have revenue producing products or services supported by the operating functions listed above.

It is useful to think of yourself as an independent contractor providing managerial services to another entity—in most cases, your employer. The employer is, then, your principal customer and is due all that any important customer should be due. As the CEO of your own business, you must manage all the activities that support the survival and growth of that business, and that serve the needs of your customer. Let's consider them in turn.

Product or Service

Just as every business must offer something that others are willing to pay for, every executive must offer a product or service that employers value highly. This might be the executive's demonstrated capabilities for planning, for motivating others, for handling the firm's assets in a responsible way, and so forth. In some cases it may be specialized expertise, such as a financial manager's expertise in the use of "derivatives" and other capital market instruments. Whatever it is you have to offer, think about ways to enhance the quality and value of your personal product or service so that it commands a greater premium. Consider what competitors are offering. Analyze trends in your industry or in technology that may undermine your value as a producer or manager over time.

Suggestion: Determine what represents "best in class" in your line of work, and then develop your skills to match or exceed this standard.

Planning

Lacking a plan, your career cannot, and will not, go anywhere. Anyone who lacks a plan will simply become an unwilling part of someone else's plan. The planning function identifies which actions are required to advance your career to where you want it to be at various points in the future. A career plan begins with clear and realistic time-based objectives. These objectives should be listed chronologically, with specific target dates for those that fall within the coming five-year period. Those falling beyond the five-year period should have parameters such as "2000–2005." Your plan will need to be flexible, given the dynamic nature of the workplace, the timing of objectives, the action steps for reaching them, and even the objectives themselves, which must be reconsidered when the environment changes dramatically.

As you identify the chronological action steps, keep in mind the resources and opportunities available within your own organization. Just as it is a mistake for major corporations to pay more attention to potential customers than to existing customers, individuals often spend too much time thinking about new careers with potential employers while overlooking the opportunities that are right beneath their noses. Potential customers are important and it would be shortsighted to neglect them. But you need to keep sight of the opportunities at hand at the same time.

Some Suggestions: Corporations generally keep their plans secret. You should too. Be subtle in conveying your career preference to the corporation; this allows you to revise your objectives and corresponding plan without being perceived as not knowing what you really want. Ideally, your plan should mesh with the needs of the organization that employs you. After all, any successful business seeks to meet the needs of its best customer(s). So should you.

Research and Development

In a speech to a business conference in 1991, Motorola chairman Robert Galvin reminisced about how his father, who preceded him as chairman, had sized up Motorola's competitive environment in the late 1940s. According to the elder Galvin, there were fourteen serious competitors in those days. Of this pool of rivals, however, only Motorola survived into the 1990s. All had disappeared—their products having become obsolete or ineffective. Motorola, on the other hand, had made a continuing set of strategic transitions over the decades into emerging product areas: from car radios to television sets to pagers and cellular phones to advanced semiconductors. Each transition was made possible by the company's dedication to R&D and a corporate attitude that supported change.

With few exceptions, companies must invest in research and development if they hope to improve current products or introduce the new ones that represent the future. For some corporations, R&D is part of the corporate religion. For example,

3M Corporation lives on the revenues generated by newly developed products. In a typical year, some 80 percent of 3M corporate revenue comes from the sale of products that did not even exist five years earlier. Take away its stream of innovative new products and 3M would wither away in a short time.

Unfortunately, many executives tend to ignore the importance of R&D for themselves. "If it isn't taught on company time, I'm not taking the course," some are likely to say. "I'd love to get this added training, but I don't have the time just now," others might assert. This is losers' talk. The modern executive must continually upgrade his or her skill base. You must be a perpetual student of your specialty, your profession, your company, and your industry. Incessantly seek to broaden your base of professional knowledge and expertise, even if you must do so on your own time and at your own expense. Corporations view R&D as a necessary investment. As CEO of your own business, you should do the same. Additional suggestions:

- Take advantage of company-sponsored training programs whenever possible. Unfortunately, not all are of the highest caliber, and those put on by management consultants are too often "infomercials" for their consulting services. Check with prior attendees if you have questions about a program's value to you.

- Become an incessant reader of trade and professional journals in your field as well as any business publications.

Recognize that communication skills are among the most valued assets of successful executives. And these are skills that can be developed through training and practice. Public speaking, presentations, the writing of reports, memos and letters, one-on-one communications, and listening become more important as executives progress in their careers. Make these skills a top priority for development.

Most research and development efforts are organized around the notion of a "portfolio" of R&D projects. Rather than putting all their bets on one new technology or product development project, a diversified but coordinated set of projects is pursued simultaneously. This usually lowers the risk to the company and results in a more robust set of technical capabilities and new products. In managing your career, you, too, need to think in terms of a portfolio of critical managerial and technical skills. Taken together, these skills will assure and enhance your employability.

Executives and aspiring managers need to regenerate their current skills and knowledge on a continuing basis if their careers are to grow and flourish. They can do this through continuous learning, which is the career parallel to research and development. As *Fortune* indicated several years ago, "More and more of tomorrow's jobs will require people who are not only skilled but also adaptable and able to keep learning."[3]

"Learning is more important to your career than any raise or promotion," notes John Kitson, human resources vice president for First Banks. Successful executive careers now must be grounded in continual learning, the widening of their spheres of expertise and knowledge. "Whatever your specialty, identify those hard skills that are critical to your profession. Learn them, refine them, stay ahead of the wave. Never let them wane," advises Partners In Performance president, Lynn Nemser.

Suggestions: If you are currently in the job market, go to work for a company that will give you an opportunity to build a broad portfolio of skills.

"*Re-pot*" yourself every few years. House plants must be repotted in fresh soil every so often if their roots are to grow. It is the same with executives and technical professionals. After a few years you will have learned as much as you will ever learn about your current job; and you will have learned as much as you will ever learn from the people with whom you are working. Find another position with different challenges and a different work group. Learn as much as you can as quickly as you can in this new environment, and then be prepared to move on to something new.

Broaden your understanding of the business by spending some time every week with a key person in another department.

If you are a marketing executive, get to know a manager in the production department or in customer service. Develop an understanding of that person's concerns and an understanding of how that end of the business works. In Japan, executives are deliberately rotated though different departments so that their understanding of the total business is continually enriched. We seldom do this in the United States, but you can make it your business to do so.

Operations

During the 1970s, freshly minted MBAs were less interested in operational excellence than in displaying a sense of urgency. Starting programs was more important than finishing them, and a relationship with the boss was more important than actual performance. Whatever success might have come from those attitudes was surely short-lived. What counts in the long run is getting work done in an efficient and effective manner. This is what matters today, and to do it requires highly organized work habits.

For the executive, highly organized work habits involve effective time management, planning, and judicious use of delegating. Lacking these, your career plans will be lost in a work situation that is forever out of control. This out-of-control situation is characterized by a continuous struggle to meet deadlines, operational errors, missed appointments, poorly prepared presentations, and so forth. All are career killers.

Suggestions: Learn and practice any one of the proven time management systems now on the market. Remember that, as an executive, time is both your most *important* asset and the most commonly and easily wasted asset—it is always winding down. You must make the most of it.

Plan your work; then work your plan. The chaotic nature of managerial work requires that you identify and prioritize the activities that must be done, and develop a plan for doing them. Many executives either stay fifteen minutes late at night or come in fifteen minutes early the next day to do this planning—before the telephone starts ringing and people show up at their office doors with problems. Without a plan and the will to execute it, your day will be taken over by others.

Information Systems

One of the traditional rationales for management hierarchies is the movement of information within the organization. Information systems are quickly replacing managers in that important function. In fact, the current wave of downsizing in Corporate America has been facilitated by the growing power of information systems. Also, information systems—when properly developed—are capable of linking the otherwise separate functional areas of the enterprise (manufacturing, sales, finance, suppliers, etc.) so that activities and knowledge can be integrated in ways that better serve the customer.

As an executive, you cannot be oblivious to voice mail, E-mail, facsimile, personal computers, data bases, and the other artifacts of the information age. These are the tools of the late twentieth century and you must learn to use them effectively.

Suggestions: As a decision maker, learn the capabilities and limitations of your company's information system.

Don't be a technology junky. Too many junior executives waste time playing with their personal computers, making their spreadsheets look better with fancy borders, spending endless hours developing three-dimensional graphics to enhance their reports, and so forth. Remember that the real purpose of computers and software is to increase productivity and use information in better ways.

Sales and Customer Service

Sales creates the revenues that make it possible for a business to survive. Customer service makes repeat sales easier to come by, while at the same time providing a feedback loop through which customer needs and satisfaction can be measured. Over the past decade, the notion of customer satisfaction and its impact on profitable sales has truly come into its own.

As the CEO of your own "business," you need to determine who are your real "customers" and see to it that their needs are totally satisfied. As a corporate employee, your boss will be the most obvious and probably the most important of these customers. You should think of yourself as an independent contractor and your boss as your best client, and you should ask yourself, am I delivering the kind of customer satisfaction that would lead my boss and my other customers to say "She's a world-class supplier! We'd be glad to do more business with her"?

Suggestions: Senior management's perceptions of you will generally be based upon very limited contact. Make sure that each of these contacts leaves a positive impression. This means being thoroughly prepared for any encounter and doing whatever is necessary to deliver total customer satisfaction.

Make yourself a valued source of information and ideas for your boss and other internal "clients." As you develop yourself professionally, quietly pass on any articles, books, research, etc., that will be useful to them. Help them to be successful in their careers and you will reap uncounted dividends.

Public Relations

Your career will never go anywhere if you keep your light under a basket. Public relations is a channel of communication between you and those with whom you wish to interact. It represents an opportunity for two-way communication between you-as-a-business and the individuals and organizations who are willing to hire and pay you.

The public relations aspect of this activity involves maintaining a broad network, both inside and outside of your company, of contacts who can help you in some way with information, promotions, or new employment. Like a garden, this network must be cultivated and nurtured if it is to be fruitful. That means that you must invest time and effort in building personal relationships, and you must be as much a "giver" as a "taker" with respect to people in the network.

Suggestions: Have lunch at least once a week with someone in your network. Learn as much as you can from these persons. Tell them what you know. Those who give will receive. You must be as willing to advise, help, and share information with others as you are to receive their advice, help, and information. Your willingness to share will rebound to you someday when you need it.

Human Resource Management

As an executive, your career success will almost surely be a function of efforts that involve other people. Executives, by definition, get things done through others. Some of these others will be under your direct supervision; some will be team members with whom you have only collaborative relationships. To the extent that it is possible, you must continually improve the capabilities of those with whom you work—through training, nurturing, careful personnel screening and promotions, and judicious selection of team members. These tasks are made more difficult by demographic changes, the failure of individuals and our education system to produce workers with solid fundamental skills, and a blizzard of government and corporate mandates relative to hiring, firing, and advancement. In upgrading the capabilities of those around you, however, you enhance your own ability to get things done.

Suggestions: The rules that govern hiring, firing, and promotion are a byzantine science, filled with dangers for the unwary executive. Human Resources departments are specialists in these matters. Make the most of them.

Create a successor. Many executives avoid creating a competent successor out of fear that they might be seen as expendable. What they fail to understand is that they themselves will never be promoted as long as no competent replacement is available. If you really want to move ahead, you must prepare someone to step into your current position. Human assets are rapidly displacing capital assets in the value creation process. If you are seen as a person who develops the human assets of the enterprise, your value to the corporation will be enhanced.

Financing

Many successful executives maintain what is called a "go to hell fund." It is a pool of financial assets that can substitute for a regular paycheck in the event of a layoff or a voluntary resignation. It is a bad idea to remain in an untenable job simply because you cannot afford to leave. A "go to hell fund" makes risk taking with career choices less risky. (And always remember that career development—like any opportunity for growth— always entails risk.)

Suggestion: Determine the amount of cash-type assets you would need to support yourself through 6–10 months of transition to a new position or to self-employment, then start accumulating it. Remember that transitions to higher level positions take longer than to lower level jobs. Some outplacement specialists suggest that every $10,000 of current salary corresponds to one month of transition time.

EMPLOYEE VERSUS EMPLOYER

Ten years ago the idea of an executive treating his or her career as a personal business—as advocated here—would have been viewed as self-serving and disloyal. The idea also conjures up the image of employees who spend much of their time either looking for other jobs or ready to abandon ship at the first whiff of trouble. As Waterman, Waterman, and Collard describe it:

> A workforce of loners roaming corporate halls, factories, and E-mail systems? . . . Should management be satisfied with employees whose only loyalty is to their own careers? How can an enterprise build capabilities, forge empowered teams, develop a deep understanding of its customers, and—most important— create a sense of community or common purpose unless it has a

relationship with its employees based on mutual trust and caring? And how can an enterprise build such a relationship unless
it commits something to employees and employees commit
something to it?[4]

For the most part, corporations today are clearly more comfortable with the idea that their managers and executives are
in charge of their own careers—even if that means that more
of them put their interests above those of the corporation and
leave in greater numbers. The concept of self-managed careers
relieves corporations of obligations they are no longer willing
or able to fulfill. Corporations also understand that self-reliant
employees who take responsibility for continually reinvigorating their own skills and keeping pace with change are equally
capable of reinvigorating the corporation itself—in effect,
keeping it apace with change.

From your vantage point, treating your career as a business
will give you a greater sense of control over your own progress and your eventual destiny. As master of your own career,
you will feel more empowered and less subject to the arbitrary
actions of a large, faceless organization.

GROWING AND CHANGING

Taking charge of your own executive career involves more
than simply viewing it as a business. A change in identity occurs over time as a new manager enters the work force and
progresses to higher levels of executive responsibility. If you
are a new manager, you must recognize that the identity you
currently embrace will have to give way to a new identity as
you move forward.

In the previous chapter, under the discussion of expertise,
we mentioned that there is a shift in the importance placed on
a manager's technical versus general skills as he or she progresses to higher levels of authority. To reiterate, technical
skills are much more important at lower levels of management, but much less important among top executives. Likewise, the emphasis on general skills increases as the
executive's span and scope of responsibilities increases.

As a new manager or new MBA, you probably identify heavily with the technical business tools you have acquired—analysis of financial reports, drawing of statistical inferences from market research, application of net present value and internal rate of return formulas to decision problems, etc. Given a lack of experience, these are your stock in trade. You also probably identify with your work in terms of what you, as an individual, bring to it. Chances are that these identities will change over time.

In her book *Becoming A Manager,* Linda Hill interviewed a set of newly minted managers who described the transformation of identity they experienced over a period of years (see Figure 4–1). Many were clearly uncomfortable with the transformation and experienced a great deal of emotional stress, while others adjusted to it quite naturally.

Hill's in-depth study of new managers indicates the stressful nature of this transitional process as individuals have to let go of old habits and attitudes. Those who succeeded appeared to have mastered four transformational tasks. They:

1. Learned what it meant to be a manager.
2. Developed interpersonal judgment.
3. Gained self-knowledge.
4. Learned to cope with stress and emotion.

From	To
A specialist and doer. Directly performs specific technical tasks. Strongly identified with those tasks.	A generalist and agenda-setter. Orchestrates diverse tasks, including finance, product design, and manufacturing or organization. Strongly identified with a business or the management profession.
An individual actor. Gets things done mostly by one's own efforts. Strongly identified as relatively important.	A network builder. Gets things done through others, including subordinates over whom one has formal authority. Strongly identified as highly interdependent.

From Linda Hill, *Becoming A Manager* (Boston, MA: Harvard Business School Press, 1992), p. 6. With permission.

Figure 4–1   Transformation of Identity

If you are like Hill's interview subjects, you too will have to face up to these important transformational tasks, none of which can be helped through formal training.

These are highly personal challenges, and your best bet for dealing with them is to enlist the aid and support of a more experienced executive—someone who has successfully dealt with them and is willing to share his or her insights and wisdom.

ADVICE FROM OTHER EXECUTIVES

By now it is probably clear that executive success depends upon a combination of traits and skills, most of which can be developed by individuals over a period of time. This success is a process of growth, change, and hard work for which there are no real shortcuts.

U.S. companies need talented, dedicated, imaginative executives who can lead them into the competitive world economy—one that is full of uncertainties, but also full of possibilities. They also need leaders with humanistic or philanthropic interests. As the century draws to a close, it is becoming undeniably apparent that what's good for business and what's good for people are not antithetical. Arguably, it may have always been the case. But now, there is a sense of urgency about its recognition and the need for a rapid response to the human issues of our time.

The human factor has always been the random element in business success formulas. Theories of human control and predictability abound, from Machiavelli to Skinnerism to Taylorism to Theory X and Theory Y. But people have persistently subverted formulas of control. Theories and formulas have never been a match for the dynamism of the human spirit. Business leaders today must be students of that spirit, not seeking to control and manipulate it, but to understand its subtleties and unpredictable nature.

Human unpredictability is the source of many management headaches, but at the same time, it is the key to creative possibilities when the positive and creative side of human will can be directed toward the fulfillment of defined needs. But before these needs can be fulfilled, certain requirements must be met, the primary of these being human dignity. Where that basic requirement is unrecognized, or where it is battered and trampled, there is little possibility of tapping the best that people have to offer. Effective leaders appreciate the importance of human dignity and its connection to business success.

Effective and, ultimately successful, leaders will be the ones who are able to work within the paradoxical framework, the creative tension between unpredictability and creativity. If understood properly, it is a framework that permits both: human dignity and business success.

Business is a microcosm—fashioned out of the textures of the social and cultural milieu from which it springs and within which it must be situated. It cannot divest itself of the very material that is its foundation. But, as a human creative project, it can transcend itself to varying degrees—usually incrementally, and it then serves to fashion that which surrounds it. Any human endeavor is both a template of and template for some aspect of itself.

The successful executives interviewed and surveyed for this book have underscored the urgency for change in how we view and do business in this country. They have the first-hand understanding of the problems faced by U.S. businesses and those who lead them. It is they, too, who are ultimately responsible for the succession of leadership. For the remainder of this chapter, we have culled our data for their insight and wisdom from which four key pieces of advice have emerged:

1. Keep learning and growing.
2. Develop a global perspective in terms of business, history, culture, and politics.
3. Always do your best.
4. Learn how to interact with and care about others.

Keep learning and growing.   The learning process is never ending. When you think you know enough, you cease to learn. And when you cease to learn, you cease adding value.

New college graduates must develop patience and recognize that their careers may not move at the pace they would like. They are required to establish themselves, prove themselves, before being given their next job or promotion, and they must recognize that there is yet a lot to be learned.

Knowledge in today's dynamic and changing world is never static. Peter Topping, from Kenan-Flagler, advises: "Realize that the challenges to be faced require constant education, professional development, and attention to building personal capacity."

There is not a single successful executive today who does not emphasize the need to keep learning, to seek out learning opportunities, and to change with the times. "Be patient. Don't set time schedules for yourself," advises Teerlink.

> Recognize that your future is dependent upon your learning as the world is changing. The executives of the "command and control" environment of the past are having trouble today. They can change if they want to, but many of them say, "I made it, I'm here and I won't change." And I think, unfortunately for them, they'll have very successful careers that will end being unsuccessful. So be patient and recognize that change is the one thing that's constant in your life and learn how to deal with it.

Learning is something that occurs naturally, as long as the channels remain open. But it surely can be stopped. Closed-mindedness can quickly stymie growth and opportunity. From Johnson & Johnson's Quality Institute, J.C. Parrella notes: "I don't know if you can just develop the ability to learn. You can learn by constant exposure to new things, and not fearing failure."

The traditional methods for increasing one's knowledge are still applicable. "Read, read, read. Never be without reading," was the advice from several executives. Read newspapers, trade journals, news magazines—even gossip rags arguably have their place. Listening to what others are saying, to their ideas, complaints, and criticisms, is also another valuable means for gaining new information and perspective.

"Never stop learning," former Equibank CEO Claire Gargalli says. "One little trick I used to use way back with the folks that

I worked with in the international field, if someone didn't read the *New York Times* at some point in their career, I almost gave up on them. One may not agree with the politics, but if one does not have the curiosity and desire to learn more, I say 'hang it up.'"

Develop a global perspective in terms of business, history, culture, and politics. No business exists in isolation. Everything, and every business, is part of a larger web of activities. Your business is part of a complex world economy. International politics, trade policies, the political climate across the globe, the civil war in some remote corner of the globe, all have an impact on your business, your work, your career. "The global economy is a central fact. Its implications extend to public policy and support for improved schooling," observes Sven Groennings, formerly vice president of education for American Express Corporation.

Executives must not look for a lifetime corporate appointment in their hometown. They have to be mobile, willing to move to another country and work with people from those countries. The most employable individuals in the future will be those able to take foreign assignments with some measure of ease and self-assurance.

Having global perspective means learning more about the world economy, and about the countries and people in which one's company has businesses or does business. History, culture, and politics should not be alien fields of study for executives. The global economy is in a state of flux. Opening markets, shifting alliances, new organizational stimuli, and increasing interdependence are all shaping the global economy. The U.S. is but one player—at present, a very shaky player.

A liberal arts education, whether acquired formally or independently, is a great asset in any business career. Naturally, this cannot substitute for a sound business education, but specializing should not be at the cost of broadening one's knowledge base. "Too much function-specific college preparation is deleterious to the global view required in the business executive," observes Marvin Roth, director of career planning and placement at Lafayette College.

As business leaders all over the world begin to have greater contact with one another, executives will increasingly require diplomatic skills. And since no company wants to fund costly diplomatic blunders, individuals with agility in cross-cultural exchanges will be in great demand.

Always do your best.   It goes without saying that success in any endeavor requires persistence, dedication, patience, energy, hard work and a willingness to make sacrifices for one's goals. Frustrations and disappointments, setbacks and sometimes injustices can be part of the game. But successful people are undeterred. "Successful executives remain committed to their aspirations and objectives regardless of the environment or times," noted one executive.

"For every great success story there are thousands of perfectly understandable reasons to lower one's goals or quit. The difference is that successful people don't lower their sights. No matter what," advises another.

The winner is rarely someone who has never lost, but someone who keeps getting up, keeps getting back into the ring, keeps looking for a new way, a new answer. Edwin Artzt, vice-chairman of Proctor & Gamble and president of P & G International, in a speech in 1988 to Wharton's Lauder Institute of International Management, discussed what it takes to become a winner:

> It's a fact that there are winners and losers in management, and most are not born winners. You learn how to win. If you don't, you lose . . . Winning in management requires an exceptional combination of attitude, skills and personal character. . . . Learning to win in this very tough, competitive world is not something that you do only when it counts. You have to try to make it part of your attitude toward life, certainly a part of your attitude toward work.

Striving to do one's best entails hard work, and this is something Vanguard's Jack Bogle stressed throughout our interview with him:

> . . . I happen to believe that if you want to realize your potential, there's absolutely no substitute for work—there's no shortcut,

there's no easy way. . . . do your job and do it well. You have to be ambitious to take on more work, ambitious to get ahead, and you should be working. I'm a believer that long hours are the price you pay for success.

Motorola Chairman George Fisher likewise places the emphasis on doing the best job possible:

Our goals as we progress in life should be to do very well whatever it is we're doing. If I'm picking up garbage, I want to be the best garbage collector in the world. If I'm designing an integrated circuit, I want to be the best at that. Learn as much as you can, but set your aspirations to being really good at what you do and not always, but most of the time, the progression will take care of itself.

Simplistic as it sounds, focusing on doing one's best every day brings renewed vitality to the job. It can be a stimulus for new ways of looking at and solving problems, a means to proactive involvement in the development of job, company, and career.

Learn how to interact with and care about others.   This is another communication theme but with an added dimension that was implicit in previous comments. Really caring about others is important because success cannot be won alone. Successful executives aren't insular or independent entities. They are very much people of and for the world, and their success is interdependent with the success of others.

From a very practical standpoint, if you want others to work toward the goals you have, and do so in the most productive and efficient way possible, you must create relationships based upon mutual consent and respect. These cannot be established through niceties or manipulations. "Establish relationships that will support, guide, or offer assistance," recommends David D. Slabicki, regional personnel manager of Pitney Bowes Management Services. The key to establishing collaborative relationships is communication at a basic human level. Without it, things go to pieces. "Miscommunication and the lack of communication are the primary sources of lost business, bruised egos, stalled careers and personal frustration in the corporate world," warns Tony Lee, editor of the National Business Employment Weekly of Dow Jones & Co. Inc.

Barriers to the free flow of communication must be dismantled. The traditional organization of corporate work into special functions or departments like marketing, engineering, customer service—what many critically call silos—represents one of the key barriers to free flowing communications.

"Knock down silos," one executive suggested. "Most companies are comprised of a host of silos that make lateral communication and collaboration all but impossible." In the past, individuals could spend their entire careers in a single silo, competing with other silos in the same company. Cross-departmental cooperation is now required if a company is to successfully compete in the global marketplace.

Communication Is a Two-Way Proposition

Employees must know they can communicate with their superiors. Executives can't afford to remain insulated from criticism. If you hear only what you want to hear, it is unlikely you will hear what you need to hear. "An executive must create an environment in which people feel comfortable coming to him or her," says Joyce Goodman, employment director at 20th Century Fox in Woodland Hills, California. "Without trust and genuine interest by the executive, creativity and growth are stifled, and if subordinates only give executives back what they seem to want, they waste people and talent."

As L. Ezrre Jr., manager of Human Resources, Hughes Systems Group points out: "Our ability to communicate effectively with one another depends on the level of appreciation we have for our individuality and the richness in the resulting diversity."

Make no mistake about the importance being placed on the value and valuing of people and the earnestness on the matter of top business leaders in the country today. Anyone who cannot, or will not, believe that this is a vital component of executive training and success ought to consider another type of

career. Top executives are often quite idealistic. They care very much about the ramifications of their actions, about the impact they have on people and the communities in which they do business, and about the human condition in general.
Jim Burke's comments:

> . . . you have to understand that I start out as an optimist, which I think is also a characteristic of most successful people—most successful people get things done because they see the world more optimistically . . .
>
> While there are tremendous concerns in the country, and there are always plenty of people who are cynical, there is basic goodness. De Tocqueville said that America is great because America is good and when America ceases being good, it will cease being great. I think that's true and I think that the public understands that. I think they see that the goodness inherent in themselves and in the whole business of community action and society working together, whether it's a business community or whether it's the community in which they live, is part of what makes this country great. I see a huge resurgence. I see it all over the country, and I think that businesses see it. All of that stuff, all of that good stuff, is increasing rather than decreasing.

Jack Bogle, in a speech in 1988 to the Financial Executive Institute, talks about squaring the achievement of business goals with meeting human responsibilities:

> For some years now, one of my principal concerns has been that growth not be allowed to deprive us of the characteristics that got us here in the first place. In my $20 billion speech last June, I described them as "our energy, our ingenuity, our will to conquer our animal spirits." We risk losing these values if we seek growth at any price . . . Grow we must, and grow we will, for as John Cardinal Newman said, "growth is the only evidence of life." But it must be not growth forced by opportunism or excess or avarice, but growth that is the natural result of serving investors effectively.

There will always be individuals who manage to achieve success on the backs of others, and many may go through entire careers without having to account for their actions. But more often, these individuals are unable to sustain their success. Executives who last for the long haul, who lead American business today and can expect to lead it tomorrow, are of a different caliber. They are the hard working idealists who thrive on the daily challenges of their jobs, and who enjoy aiding the success of others. John Young, chairman of Hewlett Packard spoke of the enormous importance of people in a speech to Japanese executives:

> The HP Way, as we call it, is based on the belief that people want to do a good job . . . and will do so if they have the tools and support they need. So management's job is to establish goals, gain consensus on them and then provide people with great freedom of action in attaining those goals.

David Collingham of Indermaur International Limited has this exhortation: "Develop your people. Give to your people. Take care of your people. It remains the single greatest component of success and the most overlooked."

Successful executives will need to strive to better understand the contributions that can be made by others, in part because they will need to rely on others to a greater extent than ever before. The talents of others must be allowed to flourish, and jobs done well recognized and, where possible, rewarded. Executives owe it to their subordinates to allow them to increase their skill areas, knowledge, and, in effect, their overall employability. Only by recognizing the value of employees can managers hope that these employees will begin to view themselves as value-adding people. The reverberations of this then start to be felt throughout the organization. This is where success begins to manifest itself.

SUMMARY

You already know from experience that just about everything in the world of business needs to be managed. Left unmanaged, most things never reach their full potential. The same applies to your career as an executive. Left unmanaged, its progress and direction will drift or be determined by others or by random events.

It is predicted that most Americans can expect to make major job changes at least six times during their working lives. How does one prepare for what seems to be a destabilized workplace? How can one begin to plan a career given these conditions? Planning has, in fact, become absolutely essential for those interested in pursuing executive careers. In the past, career planning was not a necessity. One considered opportunities as they presented themselves or, perhaps, contacted the "right" people. Bad moves were not debilitating—let alone fatal. There were always more positions to consider.

The new professional must have her or his sights set upon the idea of increasing employability. "Learning is more important to your career than any raise or promotion," according to Ed Stephensen of the Coca-Cola Company. Successful executive careers now must be grounded in continual learning, widening their spheres of expertise and knowledge. "In every area of your life—keep learning. And never ever stop learning new things, always push yourself to learn," advises Allied Signal's David Host. The vehicle to increasing employability is to foster a spirit or attitude of continual learning. Sheri Pass Lockshin, manager of career services at the Walter A. Haas School of Business at the University of California, Berkeley says, "Assume you are responsible for your own learning and the development of your own career."

One way to adopt a continual learning orientation is by finding ways to measure performance, both internally and externally. Adapting the cost quotient/cost index technique used in cost accounting is one way an executive can quantify performance. The cost quotient compares one's performance with what others, in comparable positions, but outside one's immediate sphere, are doing. The cost index is an internal measure, used to make comparisons against one's previous accomplishments and record. Some of the items that might make up the cost index are: How many clients am I servicing? Can I expand the range of services I am currently providing? How many people come to me to ask questions?

Moss Kanter, in her book *When Giants Learn to Dance*, discusses the demise of what she calls the "corpocratic" career.

That type or model of the business career is being replaced by the "professional" and "entrepreneurial" career models. In the former, it is a set of specific skills, abilities, and expertise the individual commands that make him or her marketable or employable. "Professional" careers are built upon reputation. What counts is what the individual has produced, created, or "grown" in terms of value or organizational capacity. "Entrepreneurial" careers are built upon this creative ability and generation of "new growth."

It's useful to think of your career and your daily activities as a singular business owned and operated by you. Given your training and experience, this should be a very comfortable notion. This business will have functions similar to those of any other business. And like any other business, it must be made to grow and to negotiate the world of change. These changes include the personal transitions that you will experience as you progress from an individual producer to an executive who creates value through the coordinated efforts of many people.

We cannot deny that sometimes there are factors beyond our control that may either impede our advancement or boost it significantly. There are no *guarantees* that what we do will bring about desired outcomes. And sometimes opportunities come our way that have little connection to anything we have planned.

Good senior executives and wise individuals recognize that luck factors into almost everything we do or attempt to do. ". . . Luck is a very important part of business success or any success," notes Jim Burke.

But luck should not be confused with fatalism. The breaks and the great opportunities may be beyond one's control, and of course being in the right place at the right time is a very real operator in business. But there is a caveat. One must position oneself to be able to take advantage of good breaks, or to draw good fortune one's way.

Jack Bogle says:

> I won't say that a lot of people don't get lucky, because a lot of people do and I'm probably one of them, not probably, I am—but on the other hand, Pasteur and other exceptional achievers have

said, "Fortune favors the prepared mind." You can have all the luck in the world but if you're not any good or ready for it, you're not going to get anywhere at all.

Jim Burke adds:

I think there's another element here that potentiates all of those things that we talked about and perhaps potentiates good fortune and good luck as well. I always said to people who work for me, "If you're not really enjoying what you're doing, something is wrong." Either it's you, it's the person you're working for, or it's the environment that you're caught in, or the industry, or something, and you shouldn't just sit and take it. You should figure out what it is and change it because the whole process of being alive should be joyous and there's no more joyous place to be, where you can be as interactive with all elements of society, as you can when you're in business. Business ought to be an awful lot of fun. It sounds fatuous but in fact most of the people that I know also feel this way. Most of the great CEOs I know have enormously enjoyable, fulfilling lives no matter how much bad luck they've had. It is supposed to be fun. It isn't supposed to be just work. It doesn't need to be that way and it's a common denominator of all the CEOs that I respect. They are very enthusiastic people and they are fun to be with.

The formula for success is no longer a simple one. Those who aspire to senior positions will need to approach their work lives with much more strategic sophistication than in the past. They must, to a much greater degree, take charge of their careers, their education, their learning opportunities. Business executives in the late twentieth century are called to the great task of being leaders in the reshaping of an extraordinary, complex world. They are entrusted with the hopes and dreams and futures of people, people next door and people across the globe. They must bring to their work a broad vision for these futures, the competence to make strides toward them, and the integrity and strength of character to follow through.

5

INTRODUCTION TO EXECUTIVE JOB SEARCH

The preceding chapters of this book have provided considerable information about the nature of today's fast-changing work environment and what is expected of executives if they are to be successful in the new management era. In this new environment characterized by rapid-fire change, organizational delayering, wholesale elimination of middle-management jobs and general instability, it has become very clear that employment and job security are fast becoming relics of the past.

As reengineering and downsizing continue to sweep the industrial landscape at an unprecedented clip, modern executives, despite a high level of competence and solid-performance track records, have had to face the inescapable realization that they are very vulnerable. Not only can corporate downsizing cause jobs to suddenly disappear but reengineering along with its close cousin, work redesign, can often alter job responsibilities to the extent that a once-stimulating assignment no longer proves satisfying.

Further, with the delayering of organizational structures and dismantling of functional silos, once visible and well-defined career paths are now far less discernable to the executive. Gone are the old traditional "lines of progression" that allowed individuals to automatically progress to the next rung in the department's functional career ladder. Gone too is the traditional approach to individual development which so frequently linked skills training and management development with each new rung on the promotional ladder.

Against this backdrop of constant organizational change and turmoil, traditional career planning as we once knew it is now dead. Aspiring executives now frequently find themselves in a quandary about how to structure a meaningful career plan that will help them develop the qualifications needed to advance to the senior management level. What skills do I need? How do I get them? What positions should I target for developmental purposes? What is the best route to the top? These and related questions are proving increasingly difficult for the executive to answer.

Despite this lack of clarity and growing uncertainty in career planning, one point has become increasingly clear with the passage of time. Due to the wholesale flattening of organizational structures taking place in American industry, ambitious executives wishing to get ahead must now settle for far fewer promotional opportunities than in the past. Many of the stepping-stone middle management jobs, previously earmarked for promotion and management development, have simply disappeared from the scene. They no longer exist! Thus, executives can no longer count on automatically moving through these positions as a means to their personal development and career progression.

Young executives in fact must now be content to remain at the same organizational level for much longer periods of time. Further, in order to gain the functional knowledge and expertise needed for advancement to the general management level, it will be necessary for them to actively seek several *lateral* moves across a variety of business functions and team assignments. Current-day executive career development, thus, needs to be "horizontally" rather than "vertically" focused.

THE NEED FOR JOB CHANGE

In the current business environment there are several factors combining to force a much higher rate of both voluntary and involuntary job changes for the corporate executive. Key among these factors are outright job elimination, lack of vertical promotion opportunities, and the need for more diverse functional exposure. In the present business climate, any or all of these factors can force the developing executive to pursue other employment options. Such changes might mean going to work for a new company or simply seeking a change of assignment with the current employer.

Although in the past good performers could expect to be with the same employer for a long period of time, this is no longer the case. Job elimination, along with the need for professional advancement and development, are forcing more and more executive candidates to pursue opportunities elsewhere. In fact, this trend is increasing at such a rate, it is now estimated that the average executive will likely change employers between eight and ten times during his or her working lifetime. This is up from the previous estimate of five to six times just a few years back.

JOB SEARCH AS A "LIFE SKILL"

Job movement, whether voluntary or involuntary, is rapidly becoming a way of life in corporate America. Regardless of the root cause behind such movement, it has become clear that one skill area in which every budding executive needs to become proficient is job search. More and more, the rising manager must count on job-hunting skills as the vehicle for propelling his or her career forward.

In today's business environment it is also evident that the responsibility for career development rests squarely on the shoulders of the individual executive, and not the company. Aspiring executives must take full charge of their own careers and be accountable for planning and controlling their own destinies. Don't expect much, if any, help from employers in this process.

Persons who fail to heed this advice are likely to become unwitting victims of their environment rather than confident masters of their destiny. Without a career plan and the courage to pursue it, there is a high likelihood that the individual will eventually become pigeon-holed in a dead-end job where learning, personal development, and career advancement come to a screeching halt.

When learning and personal development stop, obsolescence begins to take its toll and the executive's market value and employability diminish. Those who allow themselves to become the victims of such obsolescence are often quick to become the targets of reengineering and are frequently among the first to feel the sharp blow of the downsizing axe. It is important, then, to carefully plan career moves so as to constantly learn important new skills that will continuously enhance your value to both the employer and to the marketplace.

In order to successfully "transplant" yourself into a more fertile work environment as may be required from time to time, you will need to become proficient in basic job-hunting and self-marketing skills. In today's uncertain work environment, it is imperative to develop a thorough knowledge of the overall job search process and to constantly upgrade and sharpen your basic job-hunting ability.

Now, more than ever, executives need to view job-hunting skills as essential "life skills" that are vital to employment survival and career success. With the advent of substantially reduced promotional opportunities (due to flatter organizations) and the intensified competition for these few choice slots, the motivated young executive cannot afford to leave things to chance.

Further, these same basic job-hunting skills are vital to successfully compete for those desirable internal lateral assignments that can enhance one's general management qualifications. Additionally, these skills are a constant insurance against involuntary job loss and can be a ready tool to facilitate rescue from a less-than-satisfying employment relationship.

As testimony to the growing importance of these tools, many companies now formally recognize job hunting as an essential part of executive development. In the absence of clearcut career pathways, many firms now offer such skill training as a core component of their self-directed career development programs. In fact, job-hunting skills, coupled with psychological profiling and basic skills assessment, now appear to be the primary focus of today's corporate-sponsored executive career planning processes.

Before addressing the subject of executive job search in greater detail, however, it will be necessary to return for a moment to the topic of career planning.

A BASIC CAREER-PLANNING SUCCESS MODEL

Without a basic career plan, effective job search is impossible. It is the purpose of career planning to provide both direction and focus to the job-hunting effort. Without first understanding the type of position sought and the purpose for choosing it, the job search becomes nothing but a shot in the dark and the prospects for long-term career success and satisfaction are remote a best.

In today's business environment, where well-defined career pathways are a thing of the past, it becomes more difficult to base career planning on the old measuring sticks of job title, position level, and pay grade. Flattened organizational structures have all but eliminated the old hierarchial "vertical" organization, which was built around functional silos containing tiered promotional ladders or "lines of progression." Instead, the new flattened organization has a "horizontal" focus that emphasizes cross-functional teams, and reduces levels of management to a bare minimum. In this new organization, decision making is pushed down to the lowest possible organizational level with self-directed work teams serving as the principal day-to-day decision-making body.

From the career planning perspective, this has forced a change in the criteria used for measuring one's career success. With the shift in emphasis from individual management decision making to team decision making, organizations now see individual success linked far more with organizational and team success. For the astute executive who wishes to reach full career potential, it is important that this shift in corporate direction not be taken lightly.

The message is clear. In order to be successful in the new business climate, executives need to align their definition of success with that of the organization. Only when these two definitions are in alignment can the executive expect to receive the recognition, resources, and personal support necessary to success within the organization. Failure to make this alignment will cause the individual to appear out of sync with organizational goals and objectives, cause the withdrawal of resources and support, and culminate in performance failure.

So, as an integral part of career planning the executive must have a clear understanding of those factors deemed important to management success in the modern-day, team-oriented company. This topic, as you know, has been the focal point of this book.

Findings from our comprehensive survey of top corporate leaders and business school deans clearly pinpoints certain executive traits, characteristics, behaviors and competencies that are valued by industry and are considered to be important to successful management in today's business environment. The following summary of executive success attributes, distilled from our survey findings, should therefore prove a helpful tool in your career planning process.

As one plans career moves, we recommend that focus be placed on choosing those positions and assignments that best enable the executive to develop the attributes contained in the following executive success planning model. These are the six success attributes most commonly identified through our survey as important to executive success in today's business climate. (Notice in reviewing these success criteria that organizations now measure executive success on the basis of certain traits and abilities rather than in terms of job title, management level, earnings, and the like.)

Executive Success Planning Model

Six Key Elements of Executive Success

1. *Character*   Develop a strong moral compass.
   - Have high values, principles, ideals, & ethical standards.
   - Exhibit leadership traits that reflect positive virtues, such as courage, discipline, perseverance, openness, candor, honesty, integrity, fairness.
   - Show behavior that promotes respect, trust, loyalty, confidence.

2. *Leadership*   Be a strategic, participative, supportive leader.
   - Provide the overall vision and inspire others to pursue it.
   - Provide the strategic direction, resources, and support needed by others to achieve organizational goals and objectives.
   - Use a participative management approach (share power).
   - Motivate and lead others through coaching, teaching, enabling.
   - Stimulate the willful participation, involvement, commitment, and cooperation of others.

3. *Vision*   Provide strategic direction by defining and communicating the desired end-state to be achieved.
   - Think "out of the box"—imagining what *is possible;* see beyond the present to what *could be.*
   - Define and communicate the desired end-state (what *should be*).
   - Connect vision with strategy, practical planning, and action.
   - Rally others around the vision and stimulate action.

- Use visioning as the basis for renewal and continuous improvement.
- Have a *global* perspective—understand impact on the larger economic and global climate.

4. *Quality*   Be committed to excellence and total customer satisfaction.
   - Strive to exceed customer expectations at all times (both internal and external customers).
   - Know, clearly define, and anticipate customer needs.
   - Set measurable quality goals and motivate others to achieve or exceed them.
   - Understand how processes relate to quality goals and customer satisfaction.
   - Be committed to excellence through continuous process improvement.
   - Set high expectations and exceed them.

5. *Productivity*   Do more, better, faster, with less.
   - Continuously improve the ratio of outputs to inputs.
   - Establish measurable standards for outputs and inputs.
   - Achieve thorough understanding of processes and the relationship between process outputs and inputs.
   - Set productivity improvement and cost-reduction goals and achieve them.
   - Pursue continuous process improvement as a means to achieving improved productivity and cost-savings objectives.

6. *Functional Expertise*   Demonstrate technical excellence through achievement in functional specialty.
   - Develop high level of technical proficiency and competence in functional specialty (establish unique value).
   - Apply technical expertise to add value to organization on a continuous basis.
   - Be seen as a valuable technical resource in whom others can rely with a high level of trust and confidence.

- Achieve good balance between technical exactness and sound, practical business judgment.
- Maintain reasonable technical competency but delegate detailed technical decision making to staff functionaries (as you move into senior management positions).

The emphasis of the *new executive success,* as can be seen from the above planning model, is on the development of those management qualities and abilities that are essential to adding value to the organization. It is believed that it is these same management success factors that are critical to *organizational* success as well. From the company perspective, both individual and organizational successes are inexorably connected and cannot be separated.

Once these success factors have been fully integrated as critical components of the career process (as mandates for personal development), used as the basis for career planning, and basic job objectives are well-defined, the executive is ready to employ his or her job-hunting skills to both identify and land the desired position.

THE JOB SEARCH PROCESS

To become proficient at job search, an executive needs to understand the process by which jobs are found and to develop (and fine-tune) those skills that are essential to generating an interest in his or her candidacy. So, effective job search training requires a combination of both *process* and *skills training.*

On the *process* side, our focus will be on helping the reader to understand which employment sources have historically proven most effective in helping executives to find jobs. Surveys have consistently shown, for example, that only three employment sources (networks, search firms, and recruitment advertising) account for approximately 92 percent of all jobs found.

Experience working with hundreds of executives who have successfully gone through the job search process has consistently shown that the employment process cannot be approached in a random fashion if the executive is to find meaningful employment within a reasonable time frame. Instead, job search needs to be approached as a well-organized, step-by-step, integrated process that ensures optimal use of both the executive's time and available resources. Such a well-orchestrated, step-by-step, integrated approach is detailed in the subsequent chapters of this book.

On the *skills* side of this equation, job-hunting success is greatly dependent on the executive's ability to market him- or herself. The primary skills covered here will be resume writing, employment networking, and interviewing. All are critical to convincing others of one's ability to add value to the company and to the achievement of both job and organizational success.

The purpose of the balance of this book is to provide executives with the knowledge, training, and skills essential to being successful at job hunting. Although our emphasis is principally on external job search, many of the same skills (especially resume writing, networking, and interviewing) are directly applicable to internal job hunting as well.

6

THE EXECUTIVE
RESUME

In preceding chapters we have explored and carefully examined the important skills and capabilities required for executive success in the modern, emerging business climate. These shifts are quite real and have important ramifications for those seeking executive positions in today's job market. They will need to be incorporated into all aspects of the executive's job-hunting campaign in order to maximize overall job search effectiveness.

This chapter will deal with preparation of the executive resume and will provide step-by-step instructions for its preparation. Specifically, we will discuss proper resume format, layout, content, and presentation—the key elements that are critical to resume effectiveness. You will be advised concerning what should be included in the resume and what should be left out. Also provided are various writing tricks and techniques that will enable you to state qualifications more succinctly and with greater overall impact. But first, let's review the new, emerging executive qualifications that are increasingly sought after by organizations. These will, of course, need to be emphasized in your resume to maximize your value in the marketplace.

KEY EXECUTIVE CRITERIA

This book has been devoted, in part, to discovering what organizations now view as important traits, characteristics, and skills that are essential for success in the modern business environment. Essentially, these fall into six key categories as follows:

Higher Productivity

Today, the term *higher productivity* has taken on new meaning and a certain sense of urgency. In the past it simply meant increasing your output. In today's business culture there is a broader meaning that incorporates a sense of efficiency. Executives are being called upon not just to increase output but to do it with fewer resources. The expression frequently used to capture this idea is "Do more with less." Kingdom builders are out.

As an executive, then, when preparing your resume, you will want to highlight those cases where you have done more with less. As you review your background and accomplishments in preparation for writing your resume, therefore, you will want to take note of those cases where you have worked with fewer resources (i.e., people, budget, equipment, raw materials, etc.) and were still able to increase overall productivity and output.

Where possible, you will want to choose examples of higher productivity that can be quantitatively described. Showing a quantitative output (35 percent increase in sales, for instance), communicates far more powerfully than non-quantitative descriptions. Additionally, where possible, you will also want to show (in quantitative terms) the reduced level of resources at which the gains in productivity were realized, communicating your ability to do more with less.

Some sample results or accomplishment statements that communicate the concept of doing more with less are as follows:

- Reduced staff by 20 percent concurrently increasing department productivity by over 35 percent.

- Decreased manufacturing budget by $5 million (10%) with a simultaneous 22 percent increase in product output.

- Led corporate-wide productivity improvement task force that cut operating expenses by $35 million (18%) and head count by $10 million (20%), with no loss of productivity.

Interpersonal Skills

Another critical qualification expected of executives in today's job market is the proficient use of the "soft" management skills. As our survey work has clearly shown, proficiency in interpersonal skills has become more important than ever before and is an absolute requirement for the success of the modern manager. These are, therefore, skills that you will want to continuously highlight and emphasize in your executive resume and throughout the elements of your job-hunting campaign.

There are three principal movements in American industry that account for the increased demand for interpersonal skills excellence. The first is an organizational trend toward fewer levels of management coupled with flatter organizations and a considerably broader span of management control (i.e., many more employees reporting *directly* to each executive). The second is the trend toward a participative management decision-making process. The third is work force diversity (i.e., the changing composition of the work force to include a broader range of views).

As organizations continue to downsize and eliminate both the levels and numbers of managers, they are becoming flatter (fewer management levels) and each manager is expected to *directly* manage increasing numbers of employees, or "direct reports." This means that each individual executive leads ever-increasing numbers of employees directly. The ability to relate effectively to others and to build meaningful relationships is taking on ever-increasing importance as this managerial span of control dramatically increases.

The expanding breadth of managerial control (i.e., direct reports), exemplifying modern organizational structure, is forcing executives to give up more and more of their managerial reigns. Thus, in order to effectively manage in this environment, executives must change their philosophy and style of management. They can no longer expect to *have all the answers* and to make *all of the decisions.* Their role has thus shifted from being effective in the management of *things* to being effective in the management of *people.*

This shift in the role of executives has important implications for the job seeker. Modern organizations no longer seek "controllive" style managers, who make all the decisions and pass their decisions onto others to execute. Instead, in an effort to tap overall resources and capabilities of those who report to them (and thus dramatically increase organizational productivity), today's executive is expected to be far more of a leader. Thus, he or she is expected to see their role as that of coach, teacher, mentor, facilitator—an "enabler of others." It is expected that the successful executive will strongly believe in leading change through developing and motivating others.

This move to the participative management style requires far greater demand on the "soft" or interpersonal skills of executives. Thus, successful executives are thought to be those who exhibit the following traits and characteristics:

- Sensitivity to the needs and feelings of others.

- Easily approachable and able to engender a feeling of confidence and personal trust.

- Flexible, adaptive—able to effectively relate to a wide range and level of people and personalities.

- Openness to the ideas and views of others.

- Desire to achieve results through the development and motivation of others.

- Sees principal role as that of coach, teacher, counselor— one who develops and enables others.

- Capable of fully involving others in leading major cultural change (i.e., what the organization believes and values, how work is done, etc.).

- A desire to bring about constant change and improvement through others.

- A strong team player who encourages individual contribution but is a champion for team results.

Effective executive resumes, where possible, need to convey and highlight these critical new leadership attributes. The need for strong leadership through interpersonal effectiveness is becoming even more critical with the passage of time and the increasing diversity of the work force. Studies have shown that the demographics of the U.S. work force are rapidly changing, with white males comprising a smaller and smaller portion of the total. Minority and female composition of the work force is rapidly increasing, along with a much broader representation of persons with diverse cultural and religious heritages.

As these changes occur, the old, traditional value systems and behavioral norms of organizations are rapidly giving way to new ideas and new ways of doing things. Organizational systems must now accommodate a much wider range of values, beliefs, and ideas if the full human productive capacity of the organization is to be tapped and fully utilized. The need for such increased human productivity is evident, and the threat of ever-increasing domestic and international competition is simply fanning the flames.

This shift to a more diverse work force will continue to add increasing emphasis on the need for "soft" management skills on the part of the successful executives. They will need to manage many more employees with ever-increasing diversity of values and viewpoints, and still forge an effective team that achieves constant improvement and increased output. This heightens the need for exceptional interpersonal and people-management skills. Organizations are rapidly coming to the realization that without these critical skills in their executives, they are almost assuredly doomed to obsolescence, stagnation, and failure.

The modern executive resume must, therefore, highlight the interpersonal and "soft" management skills of the individual.

So, as you review your past background and accomplishments in preparation for writing your resume, be sure to take special note of the results you have achieved that showcase your team leadership and strong participative management skills.

The following examples of results statements may serve to facilitate your understanding of the kinds of things you should be looking for to incorporate into the resume document in order to highlight these "soft" management skills.

- Successfully led transition from traditional "top down" management approach to an "employee empowered" culture.

- Facilitated corporate-wide employee task force responsible for identification and successful implementation of $30 million in cost-savings opportunities.

- Implemented "diversity training" for all corporate management personnel, increasing management awareness of the importance of diverse viewpoints as a critical resource necessary to drive continuous organizational improvement and increase employee productivity/output.

- Directed division-wide employee Work Redesign Task-Force (utilizing "participative management" techniques), which reduced exempt employee headcount by 20 percent ($50 million annual savings).

Result statements of this type, incorporated into the executive resume, show strong behavioral evidence of both strategic and tactical abilities associated with the "soft" management skills required of key executives in today's organizations. By citing evidence of the ability to apply these "soft" management skills in the resume, the executive job seeker substantially increases his or her value in the marketplace and enhances the probabilities of a successful job search.

Problem-Solvers

As previously noted in this book, problem-solvers are "in" and executives who are *exclusively* "strategists" or "implementors" are "out." Our survey results show that modern organizations no longer value executives who are simply good at formulating strategy or who are only good at implementing the ideas of others. Instead, today's companies are in need of complete executives—those who can analyze the problems, develop the strategy, implement the strategy, and achieve the results. More precisely, lest we incorrectly convey the idea that organizations are looking for controllive-style managers, companies are instead looking for leaders who are capable of leading and motivating others to achieve these results.

The point here is that organizations are placing an increasing value on executives who are capable of achieving results. Analytical and strategic abilities are less valued in and of themselves; they are simply a means to an end. What is more important is arriving at a favorable result. Most organizations want such results now. And, they don't want to wait!

The message here for the job seeker is that you must be able to demonstrate your abilities as a complete problem solver—one who can lead teams of employees to achieve quick and financially favorable results (and, as we have already shown, with fewer resources). From the resume standpoint, then, it is important for you to demonstrate that you are able to achieve major results through others, quickly and efficiently. Therefore, while reviewing your achievements in preparation for constructing your resume, be sure to select those which reflect your abilities as a key problem solver and major contributor. In particular, choose specific examples of major achievements that reflect your ability to effectively lead others in the solution of key problems and attainment of important results.

The following examples of achievement statements should help you to understand the kinds of things you should be looking for:

- Directed team that reduced product distribution costs by 21 percent ($6 million annual savings).
- Directed quality task force that reduced customer complaints by 80 percent and product returns by 60 percent ($3 million annual savings).

- Spearheaded employee productivity task force that reduced headcount by 15 percent and simultaneously increased productivity by 20 percent ($4.8 million annual savings).

Quality Results

Organizations are beginning to place more and more premium on quality results. Further, they are less willing to accept the word of managers about improvements or gains that have been realized in their areas of functional responsibility. Instead, they are insisting that results be quantifiable. They want to *be sure* specific plans and strategies are achieving their intended results and that the results realized truly justify the expenditure of resources necessary to achieve them.

This desire for quality performance and quantifiable results has been extended to include business functional staff areas (such as human resources) where it was hitherto felt that specific results were nonquantifiable. Such functional areas are now under great pressure to develop measurable standards and benchmarks against which the degree of progress and improvement can be measured. Program results must now produce quantifiable evidence that they are worth the investment of organizational time and resources.

Along with this demand for quality performance has come the increased demand for functional executives and leaders who are not only committed to achieving improvements but who are resourceful and creative enough to develop the standards by which such progress can be gauged.

This new emphasis on quality results should also be a consideration when formulating your resume. As you historically review your past positions and achievements, you will want to take special note of major quantifiable results that you have achieved. This is especially true if you are an executive in one of the service functions (e.g., human resources, accounting, law, etc.) where, in the past, you were not called upon to document results. In such case you may want to show evidence that you have successfully made the transition to a "quality conscious" executive who values the importance of documentable improvements.

When preparing your resume, be on the lookout for opportunities to highlight your commitment to quantifiable results. Here are a few examples of results statements that clearly demonstrate such a commitment:

- Directed recruiting practices benchmark study, resulting in 25 percent improvement in company's offer-to-hire ratio.
- Led competitive practices study, establishing 5 improvement targets in employee productivity needed to achieve competitive superiority in manufacturing costs.

Vision

It is clear from survey data that forward-thinking organizations are in search of executives with vision. Short-sighted, one-dimensional thinkers are "out." Holistic, systemic thinkers, who are longer term and strategic in their thinking, are in increasing demand.

Persons with vision are felt to be the ones who can lead organizations to a position of competitive advantage. It is executives with these strategic skills who can better visualize the opportunities to create a value distinction between themselves and competition and who can lead others to realize this value distinction through innovative ideas and programs that actualize their vision.

When preparing to write a resume, therefore, executives will want to give careful thought to specific accomplishments that demonstrate their vision and foresight. Where these exist, specific achievements that highlight their skills in visionary leadership should be cited in the resume to increase their value in the employment marketplace.

The following are offered as examples of achievements that reflect vision and strategic leadership.

- Led company's initial entry into specialty chemicals market, achieving over $40 million in sales in 2 years.
- Led the successful acquisition of three new environmental remediation companies, better positioning company to fully exploit its customer base (46 percent increase in sales).

- Directed $150 million modernization program enabling company to gain competitive pricing edge and still maintain good profit margins (25 percent sales increase, 35 percent profit improvement).

Customer-Driven Focus

Today's organizations, due to their increased awareness of total quality concepts, have become very customer-focused. Whether the customer is external or internal, the goods and/or services produced for that customer's consumption must be driven by the needs of that client. Products or services that fail to fully satisfy these needs fall short of their intended purpose and do not maximize the opportunity to build customer dependency, trust, and reliance. When this happens, the supplier organization is vulnerable to competition and can lose its market foothold.

As a consequence, efficient organizations have come to value the importance of customer focus. More specifically, they are seeking those executives whose activities are customer-driven and who are constantly striving to improve the value of the goods and/or services they furnish to their customers. This means finding executives who seek to form a partnership with their customers and who involve their customers in helping to define those product attributes that will better satisfy both their immediate and long-term requirements.

Executives, wanting to maximize resume effectiveness, will consciously play to the increased demand for this customer-driven management orientation. As such, they will want to demonstrate their understanding and commitment to this philosophy by citing examples of their customer focus in the achievement statements of their resume. The following are provided as examples of how this might be accomplished.

- Increased customer product loyalty through the initiation of Customer Partnership Program, encouraging active customer participation in product design strategy.
- Directed creation of Customer Focus Program, requiring key manufacturing management personnel to work at

customer sites for 6 months to increase awareness of customer needs.

- Directed use of quarterly customer product surveys as the basis for ensuring development of customer-focused product quality and design strategies.

- Initiated Customer Product Review Team with joint customer/company participation, ensuring better alignment of manufacturing and product development efforts with customer needs.

Each of the six areas we have just discussed have been highlighted by our survey results as being essential to executive success in the new, emerging business culture. These represent some significant shifts away from the old, traditional top-down, internally-focused management philosophy of the pre-1990s and are symbolic of a major revolution now underway in American companies concerning both how management perceives its role and how it goes about doing its work.

Yes, things are changing rapidly, and smart executives will pay particular attention to these trends when preparing themselves for a successful job search. They need to package themselves appropriately to take full advantage of the rapidly growing demand for the "new" management prototype of the 1990s and beyond. The previous discussions should help executive job seekers to focus on those changes in management style and philosophy that are taking on increasing importance in the new, emerging business culture.

Having sharpened your focus on what is important to emphasize in your job search, it is now time to move on to the mechanics of resume preparation.

RESUME PREWORK

Before you can expect to construct a high-impact executive resume, there is some important prework that first needs to be put into place. Without this prework, you will find the resume preparation process laborious and time consuming and the end product ineffective at best. Although somewhat tedious, it is extremely important that you devote some quality time to completing the forms provided in this chapter. In doing so, you will be pleasantly surprised at how easy it is to construct an effective resume once this information is in place.

Starting with your most recent job first, you will need to complete a "work history" form for each of the positions you have held over the last 15 to 20 years. Although this requires considerable discipline and hard work, you will find that this effort will pay off handsomely. Not only will it provide you with the information you require for effective resume construction but it will also serve to provide you with an excellent review of your work history and specific accomplishments in preparation for future job interviews.

Before beginning this process, let me suggest that you review the sample work history form provided below. I will also want to point out some basic writing tricks and techniques that will help you to prepare a far more impactful resume document. First, however, take a moment or two to review the example on pages 119–120.

WRITING TRICKS AND TECHNIQUES

Writing style is an extremely important element of effective resume preparation. It is an important aspect from two standpoints: First, style is important in conveying a maximum amount of information in a clear, precise manner that leaves little or no room for misinterpretation or misunderstanding. Second, writing style is critical to the brevity and conciseness necessary to successfully condense several years of experience onto a few pages. If your resume is going to help you compete against the resumes of other well-qualified executives and serve you well in employment interviews, it must be written in a concise and forceful way that communicates efficiently and effectively.

Before completing the following work history forms, notice how the previous sample work history has been worded. Specifically, you will want to be aware of the following:

1. *Brevity* Note that each of the achievement statements starts with a verb followed by a noun or adjective. This practice will force you to be very concise.

2. *Pronouns* Note that the pronoun "I" is conspicuously missing from each of these statements. Since this is your resume, the "I" is understood and need not be used.

3. *Complete Sentences* Since the "I" is understood, it is not necessary to write each accomplishment statement in the form of a complete sentence. Descriptive phrases or clauses are entirely acceptable as long as they convey a complete thought and communicate effectively.

4. *Quantitative Descriptions* Where possible, use quantitative terms or descriptions to convey a greater understanding of the magnitude and scope of your accomplishments.

5. *Condense/Consolidate* Where possible, condense and consolidate what you have written, eliminating all nonessential words and information that add little meaning and/or impact to your employment qualifications.

Now, with these points in mind, proceed with completing work history forms for each of the positions you have held. Positions held earlier in your career, which have little relevance to your current job search objective, need only be described in terms of job title, company, and employment dates. Depending on your age, you may want to exclude some of these earlier positions from your resume entirely.

SAMPLE WORK HISTORY

POSITION TITLE: Vice President & General Manager

POSITION DATES: From: April 1993   To: Present

EMPLOYER: General Machinery Corporation

DIVISION/UNIT: Paper Machine Division

LOCATION: Chicago, Illinois

REPORT TO(TITLE):   President

BUSINESS DESCRIPTION (Type Business, Products, Services, Size): Fortune 300, $1.7 billion manufacturer of paper, packaging, and converting equipment

JOB DESCRIPTION:

Direct Reports (Titles):

Director of Marketing & Sales, Director of Operations,

Director of Technology, Human Resources Manager,

Manager of Logistics, and Division Controller

Functions Directed/Managed:

Marketing & sales, operations, engineering, research &

development, human resources, logistics and accounting

Quantitative Scope of Position:
(Budget Size, No. People Managed, Sales Volume, etc.)

$800 million annual sales volume, $675 million annual operating

budget, 7,000 employees

KEY ACCOMPLISHMENTS:

1. Achieved $350 million savings (46% profit improvement) in 3-year period through implementation of new business strategy coupled with cross-functional team approach to management.

2. Consolidated five-plant manufacturing division to three-plant operation with no productivity loss and 35% reduction in annual manufacturing costs ($220 million savings).

3. Increased division sales by 28% ($224 million) in 2 years through introduction of creative financing and customer payment plan.

4. Initiated division-wide program, successfully transitioning 6 manufacturing sites to employee empowered "high performance work systems" over 3-year period.

5. Led development of Quality Alliance Work Teams to assist key customers in achieving paper machine operating design capability within 6 months of installation.

WORK HISTORY

POSITION TITLE: _____

POSITION DATES: From: _____ To: _____

EMPLOYER: _____

DIVISION/UNIT: _____

LOCATION: _____

REPORT TO (TITLE): _____

BUSINESS DESCRIPTION (Type Business, Products, Services, Size): _____

_____

_____

_____

JOB DESCRIPTION:

Direct Reports (Titles):

_____

_____

_____

_____

Functions Directed/Managed:

_____

_____

_____

_____

Quantitative Scope of Position:
(Budget Size, No. People Managed, Sales Volume, etc.)

_____

_____

_____

KEY ACCOMPLISHMENTS:

1. _____
   _____
   _____
   _____
   _____

2. _____
   _____
   _____
   _____
   _____

3. _____
   _____
   _____
   _____
   _____

4. _____
   _____
   _____
   _____
   _____

5. _____
   _____
   _____
   _____
   _____

WORK HISTORY

POSITION TITLE: _____

POSITION DATES: From: _____ To: _____

EMPLOYER: _____

DIVISION/UNIT: _____

LOCATION: _____

REPORT TO (TITLE): _____

BUSINESS DESCRIPTION (Type Business, Products, Services, Size): _____

_____

_____

_____

JOB DESCRIPTION:

Direct Reports (Titles):

_____

_____

_____

_____

Functions Directed/Managed:

_____

_____

_____

_____

Quantitative Scope of Position:
(Budget Size, No. People Managed, Sales Volume, etc.)

_____

_____

_____

KEY ACCOMPLISHMENTS:

1. _____
   _____
   _____
   _____
   _____

2. _____
   _____
   _____
   _____
   _____

3. _____
   _____
   _____
   _____
   _____

4. _____
   _____
   _____
   _____
   _____

5. _____
   _____
   _____
   _____

WORK HISTORY

POSITION TITLE: _____

POSITION DATES: From: _____ To: _____

EMPLOYER: _____

DIVISION/UNIT: _____

LOCATION: _____

REPORT TO (TITLE): _____

BUSINESS DESCRIPTION (Type Business, Products, Services, Size): _____

_____

_____

_____

JOB DESCRIPTION:

Direct Reports (Titles):

_____

_____

_____

_____

Functions Directed/Managed:

_____

_____

_____

_____

Quantitative Scope of Position:
(Budget Size, No. People Managed, Sales Volume, etc.)

_____

_____

_____

KEY ACCOMPLISHMENTS:

1. _____
   _____
   _____
   _____
   _____

2. _____
   _____
   _____
   _____
   _____

3. _____
   _____
   _____
   _____
   _____

4. _____
   _____
   _____
   _____
   _____

5. _____
   _____
   _____
   _____

WORK HISTORY

POSITION TITLE: _____

POSITION DATES: From: _____ To: _____

EMPLOYER: _____

DIVISION/UNIT: _____

LOCATION: _____

REPORT TO (TITLE): _____

BUSINESS DESCRIPTION (Type Business, Products, Services, Size): _____

_____

_____

_____

JOB DESCRIPTION:

Direct Reports (Titles):

_____

_____

_____

_____

Functions Directed/Managed:

_____

_____

_____

_____

Quantitative Scope of Position:
(Budget Size, No. People Managed, Sales Volume, etc.)

_____

_____

_____

KEY ACCOMPLISHMENTS:

1. _____

_____

_____

_____

_____

2. _____

_____

_____

_____

_____

3. _____

_____

_____

_____

_____

4. _____

_____

_____

_____

_____

5. _____

_____

_____

_____

_____

WORK HISTORY

POSITION TITLE: _____

POSITION DATES: From: _____ To: _____

EMPLOYER: _____

DIVISION/UNIT: _____

LOCATION: _____

REPORT TO (TITLE): _____

BUSINESS DESCRIPTION (Type Business, Products, Services, Size): _____

_____

_____

_____

JOB DESCRIPTION:

Direct Reports (Titles):

_____

_____

_____

_____

Functions Directed/Managed:

_____

_____

_____

_____

Quantitative Scope of Position:
(Budget Size, No. People Managed, Sales Volume, etc.)

_____

_____

_____

KEY ACCOMPLISHMENTS:

1. _____

_____

_____

_____

_____

2. _____

_____

_____

_____

_____

3. _____

_____

_____

_____

_____

4. _____

_____

_____

_____

_____

5. _____

_____

_____

_____

_____

7

THE
CHRONOLOGICAL
RESUME

There are two major resume formats that dominate the executive employment marketplace. These are the chronological resume (sometimes called the reverse chronological resume) and the functional resume. Between the two, these formats represent an estimated 90 percent to 95 percent of the executive resume market, with the chronological resume representing the lion's share, approximately 80 percent to 85 percent, and the functional resume, an estimated 10 percent to 15 percent of executive resume.

This chapter will deal with the construction of the chronological resume, providing you with complete step-by-step instructions for its preparation. You will find the work history forms you've completed in the previous chapter quite helpful in the preparation of this style resume.

Actually, there are three different forms of the chronological resume. These are the straight narrative (written completely in literary or narrative form), the straight linear (where both job description and achievements are listed in a linear, line-by-line sequence), and the narrative linear (where job description assumes a narrative form and specific achievements are listed in a linear, line-by-line format).

Of these three chronological resume formats, the one which is strongly recommended is the "narrative linear" approach. Of the three, this is the format that is most easily read. By writing the description of each position you have held in a narrative style, followed by linear treatment of your achievements, you will enhance readability of the resume and end up creating a more interesting document. This approach also serves to visually highlight the job seeker's achievements, emphasizing the contributions that the job seeker is capable of making to prospective employers. Thus, the emphasis of the narrative linear format is on the "value" of the candidate (i.e., that which will motivate the employer to make an employment offer).

The chronological resume samples provided at the end of this chapter for your review are written in the narrative linear style.

CHARACTERISTICS OF THE CHRONOLOGICAL RESUME

Take a few moments to study the resume samples at the end of the chapter so that you will better understand the characteristics of this resume style as described below.

Key characteristics of the *chronological resume* are as follows:

1. Jobs are presented in reverse chronological order (most recent position shown first).

2. Format tends to highlight job and career progression.

3. Job descriptions are written in a literary or narrative format (usually a short, single paragraph).

4. Accomplishments are highlighted, separate from job description, using a linear (i.e., line-by-line) format with a "bullet" preceding each accomplishment statement.

5. The resume normally consists of the following four components:
   a. Heading
   b. Objective
   c. Professional Experience
   d. Education

The key *advantages* of the chronological format, when compared to the functional resume format, are several. These are as follow:

a. Most commonly used format—employers are comfortable with it and can find things easily.
b. Logical, easy-to-read flow with point-to-point continuity (one job to the next).
c. Highlights growth and career progression.
d. Highlights employment continuity (stability).
e. Easy to prepare—built around job progression.
f. Highlights employer names (an advantage if employed by well-known, respected company).

SELECTION CRITERIA FOR CHRONOLOGICAL FORMAT

The above-stated advantages of the chronological resume offer strong clues to the executive job seeker concerning when to select the chronological resume over the functional resume format. Specifically, the chronological resume should be the *resume of choice* under the following circumstances:

a. When you have experienced good growth and career progression.
b. When your current and most recent positions held are supportive of your job search objectives (i.e., the level and type position sought).

c. When your chronological career history shows a reasonable record of job and employer stability.

d. When you have been recently employed by companies that are well-known and respected in their fields.

Conversely, you should consider abandoning use of the chronological resume in favor of the functional resume format under the following circumstances:

a. When your current and recent positions held are not in line with (and supportive of) your job search objective.

b. When use of the chronological format would serve to highlight certain employment handicaps (e.g., lack of reasonable growth and career progression, embarrassing employment gaps, recent periods of underemployment).

c. When earlier positions and career experience are more closely related to your current job search objective.

d. When your most significant achievements occurred earlier in your career.

e. When you wish to change fields and your specific skills and abilities are more relevant to your new objective than is your past work experience.

Having reviewed these guidelines, if you still remain uncertain whether to choose the chronological or functional resume format, I suggest seeking the advice of an employment expert (e.g., executive search consultant, corporate employment executive, or senior human resources executive). In the great majority of cases, however, the chronological resume format will end up being the most appropriate choice for executives who have reasonable career records and have been solid contributors.

RESUME CONSTRUCTION

The next objective of this chapter is to walk you step-by-step through the preparation of an effective chronological resume. If you have chosen to use the functional format, however, you will want to skip to the next chapter, which will assist you in preparation of this style resume.

To facilitate preparation of the chronological resume and make this chore as easy as possible, we will divide the resume into its key components and systematically examine the layout and specific content of each. These resume components will be presented in the same order in which they would normally appear on the resume itself.

Resume Heading

The resume heading consists of your name, home address, and home telephone number. A sample resume heading follows:

WILLIAM A. SMYTH
125 Coventry Lane
Ocean View, CA 13479
Phone: (316) 775-0982

Your name should be set in bold type and in a type size that is slightly larger than that used for the text of the resume. In this example we have used a 14 point type size for the name and a 12 point type size for the address and telephone number. The text of the resume would, of course, be set in 12 point type as well.

Although excluded from most executive resumes, you may elect to include an office telephone number as well as that of your home telephone. If currently employed and you include your office telephone number, you will want to include in the cover letter that accompanies your resume the necessary cautions about contacting you at the office You can distinguish between the office and home telephone numbers by treating them as follows in the resume heading:

WILLIAM A. SMYTH
125 Coventry Lane
Ocean View, CA 13479
Phone: (316) 775-0928 (Home)
(316) 355-9797 (Office)

Generally, three to four spaces are used to separate the resume heading from the next resume component, which is the objective statement.

Objective

The objective statement is intended to convey to the resume reader the type and level of position you are seeking. As shown in the sample resumes at the end of this chapter, the heading for this component of the resume (i.e., objective) is set in 14 point, italic, capital letters, and positioned at the center of the resume. Note that the text of the objective statement is aligned with the text of the "professional experience" section of the resume, which immediately follows the objective.

The wording of the objective statement is extremely important to effective communications and to your job search in general. If worded too narrowly, it may exclude you from positions that could be of possible interest to you. On the other hand, if worded too broadly, it could create confusion about the level and type of position you are seeking or create the impression that you have not given your job search a great deal of thought.

An example of an objective statement that is worded too narrowly might read as follows:

Chief financial officer of a major corporation

Such a statement might automatically exclude you from other senior level, financially oriented positions, such as corporate controller. Use of the term "major corporation" might also exclude you from consideration for a high-paying position as a financial officer with a medium-sized, high growth company.

By contrast, the following objective statement might be worded too broadly:

Senior level management position

Lack of specificity in this case could cause confusion about the functional areas for which you are qualified and in which you have interest. It may also suggest that you are not a very specific or accurate person or that you have not given much forethought to a matter as important as your own career. This is obviously not the kind of message that you will want to convey.

Perhaps a good compromise restatement of this objective might read like this:

Senior level financial or accounting position

This leaves the exact level of the position somewhat flexible and, at the same time, opens things up for consideration in both the financial and accounting areas.

For further ideas on how to properly word your resume objective statement, you may want to study the various objective statements contained on the resume samples appearing at the end of this chapter.

Professional Experience

The next component of the resume is "professional experience." Before reading this section, you may want to briefly study this component of the resume as illustrated in the resume samples at the chapter's end. This will facilitate a better understanding of the following discussion.

The "professional experience" heading, like the "objective" statement, is positioned at the center of the resume. It is set in 14 point, italic, capital letters, and is underlined. It is separated from the last entry in the objective section by three blank lines of white space.

Review of the sample resumes at the end of this chapter will reveal that the following basic guidelines apply when constructing this section of your resume:

1. Dates covering the entire period of employment with a single employer are set against the far left-hand margin.

2. By contrast, dates pertaining to specific positions held (while with each employer) are shown in parentheses immediately to the right of the respective job titles.

3. Names of employers are set in bold type and are fully capitalized. This sets this information distinctly apart from job titles and avoids confusion concerning what positions were held with which employers.

4. Specific job titles are separated from the name of the employer (and from other positions held with the same employer) by two lines of white space. This visually separates each position and facilitates resume readability. Job titles are underlined, with the first letter of each word capitalized. Job titles, as previously mentioned, are followed by dates of employment in that position. These dates appear to the right of the job title and are enclosed in parenthesis.

5. Immediately following (on the next line after the job title) is a narrative description of the position held. This job description contains the following information:

   a. Reporting relationship (title of person to whom you reported).

   b. Description of company or business unit (including type of business, size, products, and/or services).

   c. Description of functional responsibilities (including functions managed/performed and quantitative description of size and scope of your position—i.e., sales volumes, budgets, number of people managed, etc.).

6. Although there is no spacing between the job title and the job description, the "key accomplishments" section is separated from the job description, which precedes it, by a single line of white space. This highlights this key portion of your resume and clearly separates it from the job description, increasing readability. The "key accomplishments" heading is followed by a colon and is separated from the listing of specific accomplishments by a single white space.

Each separate accomplishment is written using a linear (line-by-line) format, and is preceded by a "bullet" for emphasis.

Note the spacing between each of the individual accomplishment statements, providing further emphasis and enhancing readability.

As discussed in the preceding chapter, each accomplishment statement begins with a verb followed by a noun or adjective. This forces brevity and clarity, and adds more force and energy to the statement. Also, the use of quantitative descriptions effectively communicate the magnitude of specific achievements and improvements.

When completing this section of the resume, the worksheets you completed in the previous chapter should make the writing of this resume component easy. You simply extract the data provided on the work history forms and plug them into the format just described. Some further study of the sample resumes at the end of this chapter should make this task fairly simple.

Education

The final component of the chronological resume format is the "education" section. Although occasionally positioned before the experience section in some executive resumes, this section is most commonly positioned last. The thinking here, is that the greatest part of a seasoned executive's value to a prospective future employer is his or her work experience and contributions as contrasted with some educational degree earned 20 or 30 years ago. I strongly subscribe to this thinking.

The education section of the executive resume is fairly simple and straight forward. As the sample resumes at the end of this chapter show, this heading is centered on the resume. It is set in plain italics, 14 point type, and all capital letters.

The degree designation is then followed by school name and year of graduation on the first line. The second line lists the major course of study. The third line may be used to list scholarships and the years in which they were awarded. Additional lines can be used to show other scholarships or academic honors, where appropriate.

Other Resume Components

You will note that the resume does *not* include a "personal" section listing such information as age, height, weight, marital status, health status, and the like. The inclusion of this kind of information has become passé, and is no longer considered appropriate for the modern resume.

Likewise, the modern executive resume makes no mention of references, nor does it include such things as hobbies and extracurricular activities. These are now thought to have little direct relevance to the selection process. The modern organization is principally focused on only those qualifications which suggest that the executive has the skills and capabilities to be able to perform the position in question. When selecting executives, the focus of the selection process is on past experience and accomplishments, which are felt to be far more valid predictors of potential success than are an executive's hobbies and outside interests.

Even military experience is normally excluded from the modern executive resume format. There are two very practical reasons for this. First, is simply resume length. Due to the length of employment history of most senior management candidates, it is far more important to utilize available resume space to reflect specific experience and accomplishments than it is to list military experience. Second, showing military experience can serve to highlight the candidate's age, particularly if this is something that he or she may not wish to "red flag."

Occasionally, executives may wish to include professional affiliations on the resume, provided there is sufficient space to do so without spilling over onto a new page. This is especially true if the executive has held significant leadership positions in major trade or professional organizations associated with his or her industry and/or profession. Such listing can convey a sense of industry or professional leadership that may enhance desirability of the executive's employment candidacy.

Likewise, executives seeking senior level positions in research and development or high technology companies may wish to include a listing of their technical publications, patents, and awards. This can testify to their overall technical competence where a prospective employer places high value on such credentials.

You are now thoroughly versed in the preparation of the modern chronological resume format. Samples of this style resume follow for your general review and reference.

Sample Chronological Resume

EDWARD R. BEASON
10 Hilltop Lane
Boston, MA 13468
Phone: (617) 558-6120

<u>OBJECTIVE</u>

Senior management position in manufacturing operations at the corporate or business unit level.

<u>PROFESSIONAL EXPERIENCE</u>

1987
to
Present

YALE BOTTLING COMPANY - Boston, MA

<u>Group Plant Manager - Windsor, MA</u> (1995 to Present)
Report to Division Operations Manager of this $11 billion, Fortune 50, beverage and fast foods company. Full P&L responsibility for 4 plant, $160 million, bottling operation (40 million units, 275 employees). Functional accountability for marketing, sales, operations, and all administrative support areas.

Key Accomplishments:

● Spearheaded strategic marketing taskforce responsible for achieving $40 million (25%) sales improvement in 2 years.

● Initiated and facilitated employee productivity improvement team, realizing 43% reduction in cost-per-case from employee-led effort ($13.5 million savings in 18 months).

● Directed successful start-up of $8.5 million bottling line on time and below budget, using cross-functional team approach ($600 thousand savings).

● Implemented customer-focused quality improvement taskforce, achieving 100% on-time product delivery and 85% customer complaint reduction in 6 months.

● Began implementation of self-directed work teams and total quality programs at 3 key manufacturing sites (50% complete).

<u>Plant Manager - Wilbraham, MA</u>   (1993-1995)
Reported to Group Plant Manager with management responsibility for $40 million, 162 employee, soft drink bottling operation supplying Western Massachusetts and Southern Vermont. Managed staff of 6 with functional responsibility for sales, operations, distribution, and administrative services.

Key Accomplishments:

● Led award-winning start-up of new soft drink bottling facility, achieving first-year budgeted production targets within 6 months of start-up ($8 million savings).

- Trained all operating team and plant management personnel in SPC, and kicked off a highly successful plant-wide quality effort.

- Implemented socio-technical systems approach to management, using employee-led self-managed workteams (no first-line supervision).

Operations Manager - Syracuse, NY (1990-1993)
Reported to Plant Manager of this $12 million, 135 employee, soft drink bottling and distribution operation. Managed staff of 8 first-line supervisors and 105 hourly operators, with functional responsibility for both operations and distribution.

- Organized profit improvement committee, accounting for $2 million (25%) improvement in operating expenses in first year.

- Implemented product shrinkage control program, resulting in 90% improvement in product shrinkage in 1 year ($1/4 million savings).

- Initiated employee-led work redesign effort that eliminated 4 positions, improved employee morale, and led to renewed employee commitment to plant productivity objectives.

Senior Project Engineer (1988-1990)

Project Engineer   (1987-1988)

EDUCATION

M.B.A.,   University of Massachusetts, 1986

B.S.,   United States Naval Academy, 1980
Major: Mathematics

Sample Chronological Resume

KATHERINE W. BRADDOCK
825 Landyard Way
Woodsboro, IL 13494
Phone: (217) 633-0739 (Home)
(217) 847-9538 (Office)

OBJECTIVE

Senior level financial management position with growing company offering challenging opportunity to contribute to overall direction and strategy of the business.

PROFESSIONAL EXPERIENCE

1990
to
Present

CALDWELL MANUFACTURING COMPANY - Waverly, IL

Director of Financial Services (1995 to Present)
Report to Chief Financial Officer of this $1.7 billion, Fortune 200 manufacturer of pressure sensitive labels, adhesives, and specialty chemicals. Manage staff of 30 with functional responsibility for all financial reporting and analysis for 6 international divisions.

Key Accomplishments:

● Recommended divestiture and led cross-functional team that successfully divested $75 million, unprofitable, non-strategic business unit ($3 million annual savings)

● Implemented aggressive collections program that reduced past due accounts receivables by 40% ($1.5 million annual savings)

● Led multinational team that successfully installed new accounting information system resulting in 30% reduction in financial reporting time

● Set up financial reporting systems for new Brazilian and Mexican affiliates, training all financial and accounting personnel.

Manager of Corporate Accounting (1993-1995)
Reported to Corporate Controller with responsibility for preparing consolidated statement and and providing financial analysis for U.S. operations. Managed staff of 3 professionals.

Key Accomplishments:

● Reduced staff by 50% saving $150 thousand in annual compensation costs

● Installed new general ledger computer system for U.S. operations (corporate staff and 6 manufacturing sites) completing project 4 months ahead of schedule

● Outsourced credit function with resultant savings of $ 1/4 million annually and simultaneous reduction of 25% reduction in past due accounts receivable.

<u>Senior Financial Analyst</u> (1990-1993)
Reported to Director of Financial Services providing financial analysis support to international operations (6 countries, 9 manufacturing sites).

Key Accomplishments:

- Provided financial analysis of 3 acquisition candidates, providing recommendations to senior management.

- Participated in negotiation of licensing agreement for new stainless steel manufacturing technology resulting in $3 million annual revenue.

1986
to
1988

BILTMORE PRODUCTS, INC. - Reading, PA

<u>Financial Analyst</u>
Reported to Manager of Finance for this $120 million manufacturer of specialty stainless steel tubing. Provided financial analysis services to senior staff on wide range of projects.

EDUCATION

M.B.A., Harvard Business School, 1990

B.A.,	University of Delaware, 1986
Major:	Business Administration
Minor:	Economics

Sample Chronological Resume

GEORGE W. MADISON
433 Wedgewood Lane
Lakewood, NJ 18374
Phone: (617) 355-9436 (Home)
(617) 574-1938 (Office)

OBJECTIVE

Challenging senior operations or plant management position in progressive, growth-oriented organization where both technical knowledge and operating experience can be fully utilized.

PROFESSIONAL EXPERIENCE

1995
to
Present

DAVIDSON CHEMICAL COMPANY - Camden, NJ

Vice President Operations - Agricultural Chemicals Division (1995 to Present)
Report to Group President of this $700 million specialty chemicals division. Direct staff of 8 plant managers ($570 million budget, 3,450 employees) in the manufacture of specialty agricultural chemicals (active ingredients, formulations, and packaged products).

Key Accomplishments:

• Consolidated 7 newly acquired, high volume Vanguard Chemical Company agricultural chemical plants into existing operations, still attaining required production volume needed to support 15% increase in sales volume.

• Realized $14 million annual cost savings through in-house (vs. 3rd party) manufacture of high value-added product.

• Generated $4.8 million annual material and fixed cost savings through creation and support of employee-led, self-managed cost reduction taskforce.

• Achieved 100% of plant production capacity at underutilized (40% of capacity) plant site through development of 4 new products ($3 million annual cost savings).

• Initiated self-directed, "high performance work teams" concept at 7 plant sites in 2 years.

1979
to
1995

WESTPORT CHEMICAL COMPANY - Westport, CT

Director of Manufacturing - Agricultural Chemicals (1991-1995)
Reported to Division Vice President - Manufacturing of this $1.2 billion, diversified chemical company. Directed all manufacturing operations for $250 million, 5 plant, 450 employee, agricultural chemicals division ($140 million operating budget). Products included active ingredients, intermediates, formulated and packaged products.

Key Accomplishments:

• Led field team that played key role in successful sale of division to Dow Chemical Company.

- Directed major cost reduction projects achieving $1.5 million annual savings in 2 years.

- Relocated high cost manufacturing project to Alabama plant, resulting in $800 thousand waste cost savings annually (6 month capital payback).

- Implemented SPC-based total quality programs at 6 plants (including customer feedback taskforces), enabling first-time tracking of customer satisfaction levels related to specific product attributes.

Director of New Product Development - Agricultural Chemicals (1989-1991)
Reported to Assistant General Manager - Agricultural Chemicals Division with responsibility for directing $3 million, world-wide, herbicide product development program. Functional accountability for product development, toxicology, E.P.A. registrations, pilot manufacture, and technology transfer to manufacturing sites.

Key Accomplishments:

- Led first-time application of proprietary safener technology to acetanilide herbicide compounds, allowing successful entry into new, $50 million market.

- Developed revolutionary herbicide testing process, accelerating new product market introduction time by 40% (market entry in 4.2 vs. 7 years).

- Enabled entry into $30 million market through development of new class of post-emergence herbicide products.

Manufacturing Manager - Agricultural Chemicals (1987-1989)

Plant Manager - Agricultural Chemicals   (1985-1987)

Assistant Plant Manager - Plastics   (1979-1985)

Production Superintendent - Plastics   (1979)

EDUCATION

M.B.A., Harvard Business School, 1979

M.S.,   University of Pennsylvania, 1977
Major: Chemical Engineering

B.S.,   University of Delaware (Cum Laude), 1975
Major: Chemical Engineering

8

THE FUNCTIONAL RESUME

The functional resume, as we have pointed out in the preceding chapter, is the second most commonly used resume format. Combined with the chronological resume, these two styles are believed to account for some 90 percent to 95 percent of all resume formats used by persons seeking executive positions. Of the two, the functional format is by far the least used and accounts for only an estimated 10 percent to 15 percent of all executive resumes.

This chapter will deal with the construction of the functional resume, providing you with complete step-by-step instructions for its preparation. You will find the work history forms provided in Chapter 6 particularly helpful in writing this style resume. It is suggested, therefore, that you review them briefly and keep them available for easy reference.

There are two different forms of the functional resume. These are the "skills-based" resume (which emphasizes the knowledge and skills of the candidate) and the "functions-based" resume (which focuses on the candidate's knowledge and experience with specific business functions). The most commonly used of the two formats by executive personnel is the functions-based version. This is because when using this format the executive has a chance to emphasize his or her expertise in specific functional areas. The skills-based version of the functional resume, on the other hand, is rarely employed by the seasoned executive and is most frequently used by persons with little or no functional expertise to speak of. This chapter will, therefore, focus on the functions-based variation of the functional resume.

CHARACTERISTICS OF THE FUNCTIONAL RESUME

At the end of this chapter, you will find samples of the functional resume for your review and reference. Take a few moments to study these so that you will better understand the characteristics we will be describing below.

Key characteristics of the functional resume are as follows:

1. Emphasis is on "functional experience" and accomplishment—not on job and career progression.
2. The first page of the resume highlights functional expertise and accomplishments.
3. Specific employers and jobs held are not shown until the final page of the resume.
4. Following each highlighted major function are a series of 3 to 5 achievement statements, demonstrating specific results and accomplishments in that functional area.
5. The resume normally consists of the following five components:
   a. Heading
   b. Summary
   c. Accomplishments
   d. Work History
   e. Education

The key advantages of the functional resume format are as follows:

a. Second most commonly used resume (10 percent to 15 percent of executive resumes)—employers are familiar with it and can find things fairly easily.

b. Allows job seeker to emphasize earlier job experience, where such experience is more appropriate to current job search objectives than recent experience.

c. Permits the highlighting of job search related functional results and accomplishments, despite the fact that these occurred earlier in the career.

d. Provides the opportunity to de-emphasize or camouflage certain job search handicaps, such as:

Lack of career progress;

Lack of desired experience;

Poor career continuity;

Job hopping;

Lengthy or frequent unemployment;

Underemployment;

Lack of educational requirements;

Age.

The proponents of this style of resume argue that is provides the job seeker with the luxury of first listing on the resume those qualifications most related to the executive's stated job search objective. This highlights these qualifications and engages the employer's interest right from the start.

Although this logic seems infallible, unfortunately there are several potentially serious drawbacks often overlooked by functional resume advocates. Let's take a moment to examine shortcomings.

FUNCTIONAL FORMAT DISADVANTAGES

The functional format has several disadvantages when compared to the chronological format, including:

a. Since it is the resume style most frequently chosen to hide employment handicaps, this style resume is "automatically suspect" by the seasoned employment professional.

b. When seeing this style resume, employment professionals are predisposed to "looking for the problems" rather than focusing on the candidate's positive qualifications.

c. Since this format provides no linkage between specific functional accomplishments and positions held, it can cause the employer to become frustrated (i.e., What happened where?).

d. Lack of linkage (accomplishments vs. jobs) leaves unanswered questions about some qualifications, requiring employer to call for answers. (Most won't bother!)

e. This resume style is more difficult to prepare than the chronological resume format since it lacks point-to-point (i.e., job-to-job) continuity.

SELECTION CRITERIA FOR THE FUNCTIONAL FORMAT

Since the functional resume format has some drawbacks, executives should exercise great caution in opting to select it over the chronological style resume. Clearly, for those executives with a good record of career growth and accomplishments, the chronological style resume should be the resume of choice.

There are certain occasions, however, when selection of the functional resume would seem to be the better choice. Typically, the functional resume is recommended when use of the chronological style resume would serve to highlight some major qualifications flaw, such as:

1. Poor job and/or career progression;
2. Poor job and/or employer stability;

3. Lengthy or recent periods of unemployment or under-employment;

4. Current or recent positions not supportive of job search objectives;

5. Positions held earlier in career are more relevant to current job search objectives; or

6. Career changing where specific knowledge and/or skills are far more important qualifications than work experience.

Having reviewed these guidelines, if you still remain uncertain whether or not to use the functional resume format, I would suggest seeking advice from a knowledgeable employment expert (e.g., executive search consultant, corporate employment executive, or senior human resources executive). In the great majority of cases where you have a strong career and employment track record, however, the chronological resume will be the preferred format. It is by far the most popular resume format among executives and employers as well.

RESUME CONSTRUCTION

Assuming you have decided to select the functional style resume as your resume of choice, our next objective is to walk you step-by-step through its construction. To facilitate this process and make it as painless as possible, we will divide the resume into its principal components and systematically examine both the layout and content of each. These resume components will be presented in the same sequence as they normally appear on the resume itself.

By systematically developing each of the resume components as presented below, you will automatically end up with a completed resume product which you can take to the typist or printer. In any event, you will be provided with all of the information needed to construct an effective functional resume.

RESUME HEADING

The resume heading is comprised of your name, home address, and home telephone number. The following is a sample of a proper resume heading:

BARBARA A. ALLEN
205 Chelsie Avenue
Wilshire, NY 18364
Phone: (212) 775-7937

Your name should be set in bold type and in a type size that is slightly larger than that used throughout the rest of the resume. Typically, a 14 point type size is used for the name, with a 12 point type used for the address and telephone number. The balance of the resume text would, of course, be set in 12 point type.

You may also wish to include your office telephone number in the resume heading if it is all right for others to contact you at work. If currently employed, you may want to use your cover letter to establish the parameters for contacting you on the job rather than risk a potential embarrassment. Should you elect to include both your home and office telephone numbers in the resume heading, this can be accomplished as follows:

BARBARA A. ALLEN
205 Chelsie Avenue
Wilshire, NY 18364
(212) 775-7937 (Home)
(212) 639-7757 (Office)

Normally the resume heading is separated from the "summary" section of the resume (which is the next resume component) by three to four spaces.

Summary

The summary statement is intended to provide a brief synopsis of the employment candidate's experience and qualifications.

In addition, the summary statement is intended to "hook" the employer's interest by citing a few tantalizing elements of the candidate's qualifications that suggest the candidate would be a valuable addition to the management team.

Analysis of the typical summary statement shows that it is normally comprised of the following basic elements:

a. Years of experience.

b. Area(s) of functional expertise.

c. Statement of key skills and/or capabilities.

d. Areas where candidate can be of particular value.

The following represents a typical example of a resume summary statement:

> Accomplished marketing executive with over 14 years of demonstrated leadership in all phases of marketing and sales in the specialty chemicals industry. Known for innovative ideas that dramatically increase sales volume and business results.

The summary heading, as you will note, is in plain italics, is underlined, is in all capital letters and is centered on the page. Font size is slightly larger than the general resume text (i.e., 14 point versus 12 point).

Study of the summary statements contained on the resume samples at the end of this chapter should prove helpful in assisting you to prepare an effective summary section for your resume.

Key Accomplishments

The "key accomplishments" section of the functional resume is the focal point of this particular resume style. You will note that the key accomplishments heading is separated from the summary section of the resume by two lines of white space. As with the summary heading of the resume, it is centered on the resume, underlined, and set in plain, 14 point italic type (all capital letters).

The first functional area to be highlighted on the resume is then positioned two spaces below the key accomplishments heading, and is aligned with the text of the summary statement that immediately precedes it.

Each subsequent functional area chosen for highlight (there are usually 2 or 3) is then aligned with the first functional area. Each of these functional headings, as you can see from the resume samples, is set in 12 point plain type and is underlined.

Listed under each functional heading is a series of accomplishment statements that demonstrate specific results achieved by the executive in that functional category. As with the key accomplishment statements used in the chronological resume format, each separate accomplishment statement is written using a linear (i.e., line-by-line) format, and is preceded by a "bullet" for emphasis. Note the spacing between each of the individual accomplishment statements, providing emphasis and promoting readability.

As shown, each accomplishment statement begins with a verb followed by a noun or adjective. This forces brevity and clarity and adds more force and energy to the statement. You will also note the use of quantitative descriptions to effectively communicate the degree of specific improvements and achievements. When completing this section of the resume, the worksheets you prepared in Chapter 6 will make the writing of this portion of the resume a rather easy matter. You will simply need to extract the data provided on the work history forms and plug them into the format described here. Study of the sample resumes at the end of this chapter should further facilitate this task.

The following process is provided to assist in determining which functions to highlight in the accomplishments section of the resume.

1. Determine the type of position you seek (i.e., your job search objective).

2. Choose those three or four functions in which you have specific expertise, that best support this job search objective.

3. Arrange these functions in order of priority based upon their importance to your targeted job search objective.

4. Review your list of major achievements (as shown on the work history forms completed in Chapter 6) and select those major achievements that best support your capability in those areas to be highlighted on your resume.

5. Rank order these key achievement statements in the order of their importance to both the functional area to be highlighted as well as your overall job search objective.

6. Select the top 4 or 5 achievement statements for each of the highlighted functional categories chosen, and arrange these in order of their priority as described in Step 5 above.

7. You are now ready to insert both the functional categories and their respective key accomplishments onto the resume.

Work History

The "work history" component of the functional resume format is positioned after the key accomplishments section. This heading is centered on the resume and is separated from the previous section of the resume by two blank lines. The work history heading is set in plain 14 point italic type, is underlined, and is fully capitalized.

Study of the work history sections of the sample resumes contained at the end of this chapter will reveal the following:

a. Dates of employment with each employer are positioned at the left hand margin of the resume.

b. Dates of employment for each position held are listed to the right of the position title and are enclosed in parentheses.

c. Company names are listed to the right of employment dates and are underlined to highlight them.

d. Location of employer is listed in parentheses next to the employer's name.

e. Positions held with each employer are listed directly under the employer's name in reverse chronological order (current or most recent position listed first).

f. Note the double spacing separating each list of employer and positions held. This facilitates visual separation and improves readability.

Education

The final component of the functional resume is the "education" section. This section of the resume is fairly simple and straight-forward.

As the sample resumes at the end of this chapter will show, the heading of this resume component is centered on the resume. As the other major resume headings, it is set in plain 14 point italic capital letters. As with other major resume components, it is separated from the preceding resume section by three lines of spacing.

The degree designation, aligned with the text of the work history section, is then followed by the school name and year of graduation and is positioned on the first line. The second line lists the major course of study. The third line may be used to list scholarships and the years in which they were awarded. Additional lines may also be used to show special honors or other relevant activities related to your educational endeavors.

Other Resume Components

You will note that the executive resume does not include "personal" information such as age, height, weight, marital status, health status, and the like. The inclusion of this kind of information is no longer considered appropriate on the modern executive resume.

Today's resume, likewise, does not contain a "references" section. It also excludes such categories as hobbies and extracurricular activities. These items are considered to have little real relevance to the selection process by most employers.

The principal focus of most companies is on only those qualifications suggesting the executive candidate's skills and capabilities to perform the job. Selection of executive candidates is thus primarily focused on past experience and accomplishments. These are felt to be far more valid as predictors of potential success than are extracurricular activities, hobbies, and similar non-job related factors.

As mentioned in the previous chapter, even military experience is now normally excluded from the modern resume. There are two practical reasons for this exclusion. The first has to do with resume length. Frequently, due to the extensive experience of the executive, there is seldom room on the resume to include military experience. Second, is the matter of age. Showing military service on the resume can serve to highlight the candidate's age, which may invite the possibility of age discrimination.

Occasionally, executives may want to include their professional affiliations on the resume, provided there is sufficient space to do so. This could be desirable when the executive has held important leadership positions in major trade or professional associations. Holding such offices can convey a sense of professional leadership and accomplishment that can enhance the desirability of the executive's employment candidacy.

Executives who are seeking positions in R&D or technology-based companies may likewise wish to include a listing of their technical publications, patents, and awards. This can reinforce their credibility as technically knowledgeable and competent. Such qualifications will be seen as important to those organizations placing high value on technical expertise.

The following resume samples will prove helpful in visualizing both the format and content of a well-constructed functional resume.

Sample Functional Resume

BARBARA A. BERTRAM
1224 Terrace Place
Wilmington, DL 19386
Phone: (302) 774-1945

SUMMARY

Sixteen years diverse financial management experience providing innovative leadership in financial analysis, forecasting, and operations. A track record of successful projects and assignments involving major contributions in strategic decision-making, insightful financial modeling and analytical techniques.

KEY ACCOMPLISHMENTS

Financial Management

- Secured Board approval of $95 million in capital projects

- Provided financial analysis and leadership resulting in $30 million joint venture in China

- Implemented international cash management system increasing return on short-term investment instruments by 20%

- Negotiated sophisticated lease buy-back arrangement on manufacturing equipment for start-up operation in Germany resulting in $20 million in tax savings

Accounting Management

- Streamlined internal financial reporting system reducing details by 80% and reducing reporting turnaround time by 30%

- Identified and implemented over $13 million of restructuring and cost control opportunities

- Developed integrated budgeting process for fiscal 1996 facilitating ease of budget decisions

- Reduced accounting personnel by 50% while simultaneously raising client service levels

Computer Systems

- Lead selection and installation of financial and accounting SAP system modules improving reporting time by 25% and reducing accounting labor costs by $2 million annually

- Pioneered first computer systems-generated consolidated financial statement, integrating the financial statements of 8 foreign-based operations

WORK HISTORY

1995 to Present	<u>Wilton Manufacturing, Inc</u> (Wilmington, DL) Chief Financial Officer
1989 to 1995	<u>Westinghouse Electric Company</u> (Pittsburgh, PA)

1989 to 1995   <u>Westinghouse Electric Company</u> (Pittsburgh, PA)
Manager of Finance - Room Air Conditioners (1994-1995)
Senior Lead Analyst - Commercial Finance (1992-1994)
Senior Analyst - Commercial Finance (1991-1992)
Analyst - Commercial Finance (1989-1991)

1985 to 1989   <u>Interstate Corporation</u> (Cherry Hill, NJ)
Assistant Controller (1987-1989)
Financial Analyst (1985-1987)

EDUCATION

M.B.A., University of Delaware, 1985
Major: Finance

B.A., Bucknell University, 1983
Major: Accounting

Sample Functional Resume

STEPHEN T. DAWSON
22 Seashell Road
Ocean Beach, CA 23957
Phone: (714) 277-2948

SUMMARY

Senior environmental manger with over 15 years proven leadership in the development and implementation of solutions to packaging, plastics and solid waste disposal problems. Demonstrated ability to successfully interface with senior business leaders, government officials and media personnel on sensitive environmental issues.

KEY ACCOMPLISHMENTS

Environmental Packaging

* Implemented corporate initiative that reduced global product packaging waste by 50% (200 million pounds) in 6 years

* Organized and led cross-functional taskforce that replaced 25% of corporate packaging with environmentally friendly materials in less than 3 years

* Co-developed communications plan that enhanced company image as "environmentally responsible" to internal and external stakeholders

Plastic Waste

* Facilitated multi-divisional team effort that developed successful strategy to protect 15 business units whose products were threatened by global plastic waste legislation

* Served as corporate spokesperson on all plastic waste issues to internal and external customers, the media, government agencies, pubic interest groups, and the general public

* Disarmed potential multimillion dollar lawsuit by public interest group against key ($600 million annual sales) product line due to alleged violation of waste legislation

Patents & Licensing

* Generated $18 million annual revenues by licensing plastic bottle technology to 80 firms worldwide

* Licensed elastomer production technology to Peoples Republic of China resulting in $20 million in annual revenues

162   The Functional Resume

Stephen T. Dawson   Page Two

WORK HISTORY

1980 to Present   Dow Chemical Company (Midland, MI)
                   Manager of Environmental Packaging   (1994 to Present)
                   Manager Plastic Packaging & Waste   (1990-1994)
                   Manager of Patents & Licensing   (1986-1990)
                   Product Packaging Manager   (1984-1986)
                   Senior Packaging Engineer   (1980-1984)

1978 to 1980   Whittmire Chemical Company (Chicago, IL)
                   Senior Process Engineer   (1979-1980)
                   Process Engineer   (1978-1979)

EDUCATION

M.S., University of Wisconsin, 1978
Major: Environmental Engineering

B.S., University of Michigan, 1976
Major: Chemical Engineering
Cum Laude

9

HOW EXECUTIVES FIND JOBS

One of the failings of the executive job search comes from lack of good planning. Many executive candidates are generally unknowledgeable about the employment market and know little about the subtleties of finding a job.

Certainly this is not a criticism but simply a reflection of the fact that many candidates at this level have had little or no job hunting experience in recent years and need to become better educated about the employment process and job search strategies. Understanding of some basic employment statistics and a little guidance along the way is all that is usually needed, however, to get them on track and enable them to conduct an efficient and fruitful job-hunting effort.

This chapter is intended to provide the basic framework for planning an effective executive job-hunting campaign. It will not only provide clarity and focus to the job-hunting process, but will offer some solid advice concerning what works and what doesn't. Not only will it address the elements of a good job search plan, but it will also deal with the subject of job search efficiency, an important subject too frequently overlooked by most job-hunting guides. Not knowing where and how to look for executive positions will invariably add several unnecessary (and unwanted) months to one's job search.

163

Perhaps the biggest knowledge deficit of the typical executive job seeker has to do with lack of understanding about which employment sources produce the best results. As a result, a great deal of time may be lost experimenting with various sources that are not very productive. The notion of job search efficiency starts with first understanding how executive jobs are found.

JOB SEARCH STATISTICS

Unfortunately, there are no known job search studies that have specifically broken out executive jobs as a category. There are, however, several studies dealing with the effectiveness of various job-hunting sources that have lumped executive with managerial and professional level positions together. The results of these studies shed some light on where the executive job seeker can best focus his or her time to achieve best results.

Dick Beatty, leading job search author and co-author of this book, completed an employment sources study of outplacement firms in the summer of 1990. Utilizing the help of several of the nation's leading outplacement consulting firms, he was able to complete a very comprehensive study (covering an estimated 10,000+ persons) of which employment resources have proven most productive for executive, managerial, and professional job seekers. Survey results were as follows:

% of Jobs Found	Employment Source
68%	Personal Contact (networking)
14%	Employment Agencies/Search Firms
10%	Employment Advertising
92%	Total (all 3 Sources)

As can be seen from this data, 92 percent of all professional, managerial, and professional positions are landed by using only three employment sources. Also, only 8 percent of jobs are found using the hundreds of other miscellaneous sources frequently used by employment candidates during the course of their job search.

This study offers rather convincing evidence of the importance of these three key sources when planning an effective executive job search. If these three primary sources produce 92 percent of all job-hunting results, then why should the executive candidate bother with the hundreds of other available employment sources? The answer is simple—they shouldn't. These account for only 8 percent of job hunting results and are hardly worth the time.

Two other studies seem to support Beatty's findings. The first is a Department of Labor study completed in 1975, and the second is a study completed in 1974 by a Harvard University sociologist named Mark Granovetter. The Department of Labor study, "Job-seeking Methods Used by American Workers," was published in the *Bureau of Labor Statistics Bulletin #1886.* Granovetter's study, "Getting a Job: A Study of Contacts and Careers," was published by Harvard University Press, Cambridge.

The U.S. Department of Labor study, which also included blue collar workers in the mix, showed the following results:

% of Jobs Found	Employment Source
63.4%	Informal Contact (networking)
13.9%	Employment Advertising
12.2%	Employment Agencies
89.5%	Total (all 3 Sources)

On the other hand, Granovetter's study, which covered professional, technical, and managerial workers, yielded the following results:

% of Jobs Found	Employment Source
74.5%	Informal (networking)
9.9%	Employment Advertising
8.9%	Employment Agencies
93.3%	Total (all 3 Sources)

Despite the passage of time, it is important to note the striking similarities of these studies. Clearly all three establish personal networking, employment agencies/search firms, and employment advertising as the primary job hunting sources, with total results (using all three sources combined) ranging from 89.5 percent to 93.3 percent.

Based upon the combined results of these three job-hunting studies, if one is concerned about effective job-hunting methods, the strategy for conducting an efficient and productive job search should be quite clear. Executive job seekers need to formulate a job search plan that concentrates on the effective use of these three primary employment sources. Additionally, they will want to adapt and employ specific strategies that will enable them to fully exploit all of them.

JOB SEARCH EFFICIENCY

Focusing job-hunting efforts on these three employment sources will serve to shorten the length of the job search process. Equally important to job search efficiency, however, is the *sequence* in which these sources are used as well as the job search methods used by the executive job seeker to fully exploit these key employment sources.

This chapter is written with the principles of *efficient* job search in mind. The sequence of the job search plan, as presented in this chapter, is the same sequence you will want to follow when both planning and executing your job-hunting strategy. Additionally, the methods for exploiting the three key employment sources (as presented in this chapter) are time-proven strategies that are known to work and will work for you as well.

If both the sequence and specific methods presented here are closely followed, our experience suggests you will conduct a far shorter and more efficient job search. Co-author Dick Beatty has been experimenting with the use of many of these strategies in executive job search for the last several years. Specifically, senior executives (earning over $100,000 per year) using this approach and closely following the recommendations offered here have averaged five months to successfully conclude their job search. This is in contrast with the frequently reported standard of over ten months for persons whose earnings are at this six-figure level.

Therefore, as an executive employment candidate, you have the opportunity to directly benefit from the results of our learning by following the overall job-hunting strategies described in this chapter. Doing so will take the "trial and error" out of the job search process and provide the necessary direction, focus, and efficiency required for a hard-hitting and far shorter job-hunting campaign.

SEARCH FIRMS AND EMPLOYMENT AGENCIES

The first of the three major job-hunting sources with which you will need to concern yourself is search firms/employment agencies. As shown in the previously cited employment studies, this job-hunting source accounts for between 12 percent and 14 percent of all jobs landed by the job seeker.

The reason for focusing attention on this job-hunting source first has to do with the fact that this is the one source that can be most fully exploited early in your job-hunting plan. Specifically, by using a direct mail approach, the executive job seeker can contact several hundred search firms within the first couple of weeks of the job search.

It is important to realize that attempting to contact executive search consultants directly by phone (unless you already have an established relationship) is futile and can waste considerable time. In fact, usually, these consultants have set up an elaborate network of barriers specifically for the purpose of screening out calls of this type and to jealously guard their time. Their fortress may be impenetrable and you will waste considerable time even if you are lucky enough to have either the "connections" or the "smoothness" to penetrate their defenses and energy enough to attempt making it through their well-contrived net. The probabilities are incredibly high that your call will still prove fruitless.

Here is the logic behind our recommendation that you avoid the temptation to call these firms. First, each executive search consultant can normally only handle and average of four to six executive search assignments at any given point in time (even with excellent research and administrative support). Against this backdrop, you now need to ask yourself the following question. What is the probability that a particular consultant will happen to have an executive search assignment:

a. In my occupational area?
b. At my level?
c. In my industry?
d. In my preferred geography?
e. At my compensation level?
f. Requiring exactly my qualifications and experience?
g. On the given day I make my phone call?

Such probabilities are *remote* at best!

This being the case, there is really no point to using the telephone as the "media of choice" to reach these consultants. Instead, your objectives are going to be far better served by using the mail. Besides, direct mail will enable you to reach many more of them and in a far shorter period of time.

Following preparation of your resume, therefore, the first step in your job-hunting campaign should be to make a sizeable direct mailing to key executive search firms. It is suggested that this mailing typically contain over 500 such firms. Our experience has shown that such mailings will generally yield a 2 percent to 3 percent return. A mailing of 500 to 1,000 pieces, therefore, would expect to produce somewhere between 10 to 30 positive responses. What a great way to kick start your job search!

Importantly, from the job-hunting efficiency standpoint, this mailing is something that can be accomplished within the first week or so of your job search. And, it will be out there quietly working on your behalf while you simultaneously focus your efforts on using the other key employment sources (networking and employment advertising). Positioning this mailing at the beginning of your job search will enable you to quickly optimize this important employment source, with good prospects for generating employment interviews and job offers within four to six weeks of the inception of your job search effort.

The simple ingredients for conducting such a mail campaign are three. These are:

1. A good resume;
2. A list of search firms; and
3. A solid cover letter.

We have already covered the topic of resume preparation in Chapters 6 through 8. Our current focus, therefore, needs to be on developing a list of target search firms and the construction of a good broadcast cover letter for use with the mailing. Let's deal with the mailing list first.

The best known source for compiling a target list of executive search firms is the *Directory of Executive Recruiters* (Personal Edition), published by Kennedy & Kennedy, Inc. This publication contains over 4,000 main and branch office locations of both retained executive search firms and employment agencies (contingency firms). The directory provides a breakout of these two types of firms, with the contingency firms listed in a section separate from the "retainer only" firms.

Firms are listed in the directory alphabetically, including name, address, and key contacts. The directory also includes a brief description of each firm's specialty (e.g., marketing, manufacturing, accounting, etc.) as well as a minimum salary cutoff reflecting the level of positions handled. Indexes include further breakouts by geography, industry, and functional specialization. The directory contact information can be found at most major bookstores or can be purchased directly by contacting the publisher:

Kennedy & Kennedy, Inc.
Templeton Road
Fitzwilliam, NH 03447
Phone: (603) 585-6544

Current price of the directory is about $40. Computer versions of the directory are also available from the publisher, which may make it easier for you to select firms, download to a computer disc, and prepare a mail merge.

A second, more limited source of executive search firm listings is *AESC Membership Directory,* published by the Association of Executive Search Consultants. This directory lists over 100 member firms in alphabetical order (including all branch offices). It includes the firm's name, address, and phone number for both the corporate and the branch offices. Members are retained firms only (no contingency firms) and focus on filling management and executive positions paying annual salaries at the six figure or over level. Several have minimum salary cutoffs of $125,000 or higher and will not touch assignments for positions paying less than the cutoff amount. These firms are considered by most employment professionals to be the "blue chip" firms of the executive search profession. Many have overseas as well as domestic office locations. This association directory can be obtained from the following:

Association of Executive Search Consultants
230 Park Avenue, Suite 1549
New York, NY 10169
Phone: (212) 949-9556

When choosing firms for inclusion in your mailing list, if you are seeking a senior level executive position paying over $100,000, I would strongly suggest that you select only retainer-based firms. Firms that work on a contingency fee basis only are not nearly as likely to be handling assignments at this level than are the retainer firms.

If you are seeking a position paying in the $70,000 (or lower) to $100,000 range, some combination of both retainer-based and contingency firms is very appropriate. Obviously, the lower the pay, the more you should be targeting contingency firms for purposes of your resume mailing. Now that you have the means to acquire a comprehensive listing of search firms for your mailing, you will need an effective cover letter.

A sample cover letter has been provided on page 172 for your review and reference. This is representative of the kind of letters that have produced good results for hundreds of other executives who have made successful search firm mailings. Should you need additional help with your cover letter, however, let me suggest that you pick up a copy of *The Perfect Cover Letter* (Wiley) or *175 High-Impact Cover Letters* (Wiley) at your local bookstore. Both provide numerous sample cover letters that can be used as guidelines for letters that will produce good results.

At this point, you have the essentials required to make an effective mailing. As previously mentioned, however, you will want to initiate this important job-hunting strategy at the onset of your job search. An effective mailing of this type can do much to get your job search into full gear quickly and could well result in one or more job offers only weeks into your job-hunting campaign.

Before leaving the subject of search firm mailings, it is worthwhile to cover one final point. It is important to realize that, in the field of executive search, the average life cycle of a single search assignment is only three to four months. This means that executive assignments currently handled by these firms will normally be filled in three to four months, with the firms then handling a complete new slate of search assignments. The point is that, if your initial attempt proves unsuccessful, you should plan to repeat this exact same mailing three to four months later. We have witnessed numerous cases where, despite an unsuccessful first mailing, the second mailing (to the same firms) produced several interesting job opportunities.

EMPLOYMENT ADVERTISING

Effective job search requires a comprehensive employment advertising strategy as an integral part of the job-hunting plan. Employment advertising, as you may recall, accounts for an estimated 10 percent to 14 percent of employment results.

Sample Executive Search Cover Letter

LINDA M. SMITH
125 Coventree Place
Wayne, PA 19238

May 22, 1996

Mr. William Madison
Senior Partner
Madison & Associates
20 Towerview Place
Chicago, IL 18374

Dear Mr. Madison:

Perhaps one of your clients could use a successful, accomplished senior-level executive in Operations management.

I hold an M.S. degree in Industrial Management from Penn State University and have over 20 years of experience in Operations, with over 15 years in responsible management positions. As Vice President of Operations for the Warring Corporation, a $500 million manufacturer of specialty pumps for the chemical industry, I manage a staff of 35 professionals and direct all manufacturing operations at 6 plant sites.

In my current position, I have contributed over $70 million of annual cost savings in the last 4 years alone through several innovative programs which I initiated and directed. These include major programs in Total Quality Management, Just-in-Time Management, and cross-functional, self-directed work teams. I take pride in staying abreast of new developments in the Operations field, and am quick to apply the latest thinking and technology in bringing continuous improvement to the functions I manage.

Should one of your clients be seeking an innovative Operations executive with a demonstrated track record of cost savings and continuous improvement, perhaps you will give me a call. I have enclosed a copy of my resume for your reference.

Should you wish to reach me, I can be contacted during the business day at (315) 477-0896 on a confidential basis.

Thank you for your consideration.

Sincerely,

Linda M. Smith

Linda M. Smith

Enclosure

Often, employment books and job-hunting guides simply focus on "how to answer an employment ad" rather than educating readers on strategies for making full use of this important employment resource. In this case, we will focus on how to optimize this resource.

In order to fully exploit the potential of recruitment advertising as an important factor in your job search, we recommend implementation of a five-point strategy. This strategy is comprised of the following elements:

1. National Strategy;
2. Target Geography Strategy;
3. Target Occupational Strategy;
4. Target Industry Strategy; and
5. Industry Cluster Strategy.

Each of these strategies is discussed in some detail below.

National Advertising Strategy

Frequently, persons seeking an executive position will use only one or two key national newspapers (such as the *New York Times* or *The Wall Street Journal*) and practically ignore other important media. Such an approach barely scratches the surface and leaves a good portion of the national employment market practically untouched. It can be rather short-sighted and does not allow the executive to make effective use of advertising in finding employment. Instead, a far more comprehensive approach is recommended, if advertising is to be fully exploited as an important job-hunting vehicle.

Employment professionals have long known that the national employment market is best reached by advertising in certain regional newspapers, many of which have strong regional (and national) circulation. These papers and their respective telephone numbers (as we go to press) are:

1. *Boston Globe*   1-800-622-6631
2. *Wall Street Journal*   1-800-237-7100

   3. *New York Times*   1-800-631-2580
   4. *Philadelphia Inquirer*   1-215-854-2000
   5. *Baltimore Sun*   1-800-829-8000
   6. *Washington Post*   1-800-627-1150
   7. *Atlanta Journal*   1-404-522-4141
   8. *Cleveland Plain Dealer* 1-216-344-4080
   9. *Chicago Tribune*   1-800-972-9515
  10. *Houston Chronicle*   1-713-220-7211
  11. *Dallas Morning News*   1-800-431-0010
  12. *Denver Post*   1-800-543-5543
  13. *Los Angeles Times*   1-800-528-4637
  14. *San Francisco Chronicle* 1-415-777-1111
  15. *Seattle Times*   1-206-464-2111

These are the key national publications targeted by both corporate employment executives and executive search firms for recruitment of candidates for executive positions. As part of your job-hunting strategy, therefore, it is important that you subscribe to the Sunday edition of some, if not all, of these important publications. (Note: *The Wall Street Journal,* of course, is only published on weekdays.)

Beyond the newspapers listed above, there are two additional specialty newspapers that you will probably also want to obtain. These are:

The National Ad Search

This weekly tabloid is a compilation of employment want ads from seventy-two key newspapers across the United States. Each week, over 2,000 ads are clipped, indexed, and arranged into 42 executive, professional, and technical categories for quick, easy reference. This weekly tabloid can be ordered by contacting National Ad Search, Inc., P.O. Box 2083, Milwaukee, WI 53101 (Phone toll-free: 1-800-992-2832).

The National Business Employment Weekly

This is a weekly tabloid published by *The Wall Street Journal* and is readily available at most newsstands and major drugstores. It is a compilation of all want ad advertising run in the four regional editions of *The Wall Street Journal* during the past week.

Both of these newspapers can be excellent supplements to the other advertising sources used in your job search. Since many of these ads are already a week old when they are published, however, it is important for you to respond promptly to any ad that is of interest to you.

Target Geography Strategy

Assuming you have certain geographical preferences, you may want to supplement your national advertising strategy with one that focuses more narrowly on the specific geographical area you have targeted for purposes of your job search. This can be accomplished as follows.

Using a map of the United States and a yellow highlighter, start by highlighting those areas of the country that you have designated as your geographical preferences. Then, using a *Rand McNally Road Atlas* (available at most book stores), identify all cities within your targeted area having populations greater than 100,000.

Fortunately, the *Rand McNally Road Atlas* makes this task pretty easy since it provides a complete listing of all such major cities. These are listed on a state-by-state basis at the back of the atlas. Population figures are also provided for each city, so it is easy to quickly scan the information provided and spot the larger cities you wish to target.

A fast telephone call to Information in target cities will allow you to quickly identify the principal newspapers and the telephone numbers of their subscription departments. You will want to order the Sunday edition, since it is usually this edition (rather than the daily editions) that contains the bulk of the employment classified ads.

Target Occupational Strategy

An important advertising strategy often overlooked by the job seeker is the "target occupational" strategy. This strategy has, as its main focus, the occupational (business functional) specialty of the executive employment candidate.

Corporate employment professionals and executive recruiters know there are certain key journals and newsletters that are well read by the type of professional they are attempting to recruit with their ad (i.e., marketing, manufacturing, accounting, finance, human resources). Most, although not all, of these publications are published by the professional associations to which these executives belong. Others, however, may be published by outside publishing sources.

Because of the popularity of these key newsletters and journals as effective recruitment advertising vehicles in reaching highly targeted audiences, they should become a standard part of the executive's job search library and read religiously. Many ads appearing in these professional journals and newsletters will simply not appear in newspapers.

If you are uncertain about which journals to get, let me suggest the following process to assist in their identification. All you will need is access to the *Encyclopedia of Associations,* which is available in most good public or business libraries.

1. Using the "key word index," identify the associations most closely related to your area of functional specialization.

2. From the association description provided in the encyclopedia, secure the telephone number of the association's national office.

3. Call one or more of the key association officers (often identified in the encyclopedia) and ask them to assist you in identifying the key publications most frequently targeted by employers and search firms/employment agencies for recruitment of executives with your professional specialty.

A half hour or so of basic research and couple of phone calls is normally all that is required to identify and order the important publications. Armed with a credit card and a Federal Express number, you can usually have the most recent edition of these publications on your desk by the following business day.

Target Industry Strategy

Another employment advertising component frequently over-looked by the novice job seeker is the "target industry" strategy. The focal point of this strategy is the specific industry (or industries) targeted by the executive for purposes of his or her job search. These industries are the ones most likely to have an interest in the executive's credentials.

In this case, the objective of the job hunter's research will be the identification of the journals and newsletters published by the industry associations. These publications frequently contain recruitment advertising for positions in that industry. It therefore makes good sense for the executive job seeker to subscribe to these publications as well.

The process for identifying and subscribing to these "industry-specific" publications is identical to that used for identifying publications that focus on occupational special-ties. Since the research process used to do this has already been described in detail, there is no point repeating it here. The only difference, of course, is that the focus in this case is on using the "key word index" of the *Encyclopedia of Associations* to identify those industry or trade associations most closely allied with the industries that you have targeted for purposes of your job search.

Industry Cluster Strategy

The final element of an effective employment advertising job-hunting strategy is the "industry cluster" strategy.

Employment professionals (who focus most of their recruiting efforts on specific industries) have long been aware of the concept of "industry clustering." By *industry clustering,* I mean the tendency for most industries to cluster in certain geographical areas. For example, the paper industry has a heavy concentration in the Fox River Valley in the state of Wisconsin. As another example, the city of Philadelphia is a major cluster point for the pharmaceutical industry.

By studying the "geographical cluster patterns" of the industries in which they specialize and have targeted for purposes of job search, employment professionals are often able to target key newspapers that provide the best geographical coverage of the companies from which they wish to recruit. Such newspapers, therefore, are often replete with the classified want ads of companies wishing to hire persons from those industries.

As an executive seeking employment, therefore, you will want to identify and subscribe to the Sunday editions of these same newspapers. After some brief analysis of the geographic concentrations of your target industries, you will want to select those newspapers offering wide circulation and readership in the geographical areas where your target industry is most concentrated. A way to shortcut the research part of this process is to contact major national advertising firms that specialize in recruitment advertising. They make a living identifying these patterns and can quickly help you to identify the key publications that you want.

Three of the major advertising firms offering recruitment advertising specialization are Bernard Hodes, Nationwide Advertising, and Equitable Advertising. Check the Yellow Pages of any major metropolitan area for the branch offices of these advertising firms. With an imaginative approach, you should be successful in obtaining the information you need with little or no effort on your part.

As you can see, the comprehensive, five-point advertising strategy we have recommended in this chapter will allow you to more fully utilize this important employment source as an integral part of your overall job-hunting plan. Since employment advertising is the second most productive employment source, implementation of such strategy is bound to improve the overall success of your job-hunting effort.

ANSWERING THE EMPLOYMENT AD

In addition to having a broad strategy designed to capture important ads related to your job search, it is important that you are proficient in answering these advertisements as well. Designing an effective advertising response cover letter therefore becomes an important job-hunting skill.

The first step in designing an advertising response letter is to study the ad to determine position requirements. The next step is to analyze your qualifications to determine which of the employer's requirements you satisfy. The cover letter must then be designed in such a way as to focus the reader's attention on the similarities between your specific qualifications and the stated requirements of the position (a comparison most employers will appreciate).

One way to facilitate this comparison is to employ the Ben Franklin Balance Sheet approach. To use this process, simply draw a line down the center of a clean sheet of paper. Label the left column, Employer's Requirements and the right column, My Qualifications.

Now carefully read the advertisement, listing the specific candidate qualifications required by the employer in the left-hand column. Where possible, list the most important qualifications first followed by those less important.

Review of the specific wording chosen by the employer in the advertisement can often yield some tangible clues about qualifications that are of particular interest to the employer. Most ads are slanted to emphasize the need for a particular strength in a given area. Careful reading of the ad may reveal what that area is. Be particularly alert for key words and phrases commonly used to convey special interest in a specific area. Examples are:

Required;

Must have;

Must be;

Is required;

Highly desirable;

Must be thoroughly versed in (knowledgeable of);

Very desirable; and

Should be strong in.

These and similar words and expressions offer strong clues about the candidate qualifications of most interest to the employer. Those qualifications of greatest interest should be given priority and listed first on the "balance sheet."

Now complete the right side of the Ben Franklin Balance Sheet by listing those qualifications you possess that correspond to the employer's requirements. These should, of course, be listed in a linear fashion next to the employer's qualifications so as to facilitate a direct comparison. Once this analysis is complete, you are ready to construct your cover letter.

Essentially, there are two recommended letter formats for responding to any employment ad. These are the "linear comparison" and the "literary comparison." A brief explanation of each follows.

The Linear Comparison

The linear approach is most recommended when you have "most" if not all of the qualifications sought by the employer. When using the linear comparison, the general approach is to begin by stating your belief that you are well-qualified for the position. This statement is then followed by a line-by-line delineation of your qualifications that directly relate to the specific requirements stated in the ad. The following examples will illustrate use of this linear comparison technique:

Example A

Careful review of your requirements suggests that I am well suited to the position of Employment Manager, as described in your advertisement. Please consider the following:

- M.S. degree in Industrial Psychology from Michigan State;
- 5 years' management experience in corporate employment;
- thoroughly versed in assessment methodology;
- heavy technical employment experience;
- experienced in establishing functional benchmarks;
- strong interpersonal skills.

Example B

My credentials would appear to be an excellent match for the position of Director of Operations, as supported by the following:

- M.S. degree, Industrial Management, Cornell University;
- 15 years' paper industry experience;
- 5 years' senior plant management position in Operations;
- strong participative management orientation;
- 3 years' experience in socio-technical systems culture;
- solid background in Total Quality Management.

In each example, the factors listed in the linear comparison address a specific requirement listed by the employer in the advertisement. These can be directly lifted from the My Qualifications side of the Ben Franklin Balance Sheet. Such a linear approach increases readability and facilitates a direct comparison of candidate qualifications with the employer's requirements.

The Literary Comparison

The literary approach is recommended when only *some* of the employer's requirements are met. In such cases, use of the literary format (versus the linear approach) will make it less easy for the employer to spot the missing qualifications. The linear format, on the other hand, would highlight these deficits and put you at a disadvantage.

When using the literary comparison, repeat a portion of the advertisement in your cover letter and then follow with a short description of your related qualifications. This approach facilitates comparison with requirements set forth by the employer in the recruitment ad and effectively highlights your qualifications to fill the position.

The following examples will further illustrate this technique:

Example A

Your ad states that you are seeking a "Ph.D. polymer chemist with over 10 years polyurethane foam product development."

I hold a Ph.D. in Polymer Chemistry from the University of Delaware and have been employed as a Product Development Specialist for 12 years in polyurethane product development.

Example B

According to your ad, you are seeking a "Senior Project Engineer with a degree in Mechanical Engineering and over 8 years experience in paper machine project engineering."

I hold an M.S. in Mechanical Engineering from the University of Michigan and have been employed as a paper machine project engineer with Filmore Paper Company since 1985. I have served as the Lead Engineer on several projects, including a highly successful $20 million rebuild of a twin-wire tissue machine.

Before departing the subject of employment advertising, there is one final point to be made. In the interest of conserving valuable job search time, do not read employment advertisement during the daytime or early evening hours. These hours can be used far more productively for employment networking (our next topic). Instead, read and respond to classified want ads only during late evening hours or weekends. In this way you will be devoting "prime time" to the most productive of the key employment sources—networking.

NETWORKING

As shown in the survey data discussed at the beginning of this chapter, employment networking is by far the most productive of the three major employment sources. Accounting for an estimated 68 percent to 75 percent of all professional and managerial positions found, this source is *the primary source* for landing executive positions. In fact, although there is no definitive study to support this assertion, it is believed that personal networking, as a job search technique, plays an increasingly important role the higher one is on the executive ladder.

In order to understand why the networking process has proven to be such a powerful job-hunting strategy, it is important to understand the basic principles that underlie its success. Let's take a moment or two to examine these.

The first principle to understand, when attempting to grasp the importance of networking, is to realize it is an exponential process. By *exponential,* we mean that it multiplies itself and increases geometrically as the process goes along. To visually illustrate this concept, consider the following diagram of how the process works:

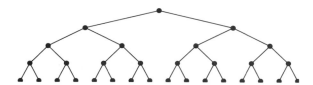

The mathematical (exponential) progression of networking works very much like classic biological cell division or the familiar chain letter concept. Starting with a single personal contact, and acquiring the names of two additional persons from that single source, the number of personal contacts is immediately doubled. Then, contacting each of the resulting two contacts and requesting of each the names of two personal contacts, the original single contact multiplies to four. Requesting two contact names from each of these four persons, there are then eight new contacts. If this process is continued, it is quite possible to geometrically expand the pool of contacts to several hundred persons within a fairly short time frame.

Thus, like cell division, the networking process allows you to substantially expand a small group of personal, direct contacts to a very sizable group of contacts, all of whom become active (at various levels of participation) in helping you with your job search. This process has the cumulative effect of considerably multiplying your job search efforts, substantially increasing the probability of success.

The second underlying principle that accounts for the success of the networking process is the sense of social obligation that is created by the personal referral, which is the thread that holds the chain together and makes the process work.

When making a networking call to a new contact, simply saying that you were referred to that contact by someone they know creates a sense of social obligation to respond to your needs. Not responding would be tantamount to letting a friend down, something that is socially taboo.

So, by managing the networking process well and using personal referral for expanding your pool of contacts, it is quite possible to recruit a virtual army of people who are willing to provide at least minimal assistance with your job search effort. The power of this group and their network of social and business acquaintances can be a formidable force in assisting you in your efforts. The statistical job-finding results of the networking process are well-documented and provide convincing evidence that this is the case.

Fear and Embarrassment

The two main deterrents to effective networking that typically cause the novice networker a sense of paralysis are fear and embarrassment. First, there is the fear of rejection, that is, someone will refuse to help you. And, second, there is the initial feeling of awkwardness and embarrassment associated with asking others for help. Both these barriers need to be removed early in the job-hunting process, so that the executive job seeker can get on with using the networking process.

The fear of being rejected (i.e., others refusing to help you) is completely unfounded. The best evidence of this is the fact that between 68 percent and 75 percent of all jobs are found through the networking process. This simply wouldn't happen if people weren't willing to help one another. Instead, networking would account for perhaps only 1 percent or 2 percent of employment results.

As further evidence of the fact that most people are willing to help others, consider some of the news stories frequently seen in the newspapers and on television. It is not uncommon to hear stories of complete strangers risking their lives to help others whom they don't even know. People will run into burning buildings or leap into flood-swollen waters to save another's life, whether or not they know them. They give this little or no thought. They just act! Certainly helping someone with their job search is far less threatening.

Finally, in the several years that we have been associated with outplacement consulting and the job search process (where most of the focus has been on the use of networking), we can probably count on one hand (minus three fingers) the number of times people have refused to provide some kind of assistance in response to a networking call. And we have been in a position to witness thousands of networking calls. So, believe us when we say that there is absolutely no reason to fear rejection when making job search networking contacts.

Second, there is the matter of embarrassment. It is quite common for those networking for the first time to feel an initial sense of embarrassment. Calling someone else to ask them for assistance with your job search is something that doesn't quite come naturally for most. Most of us take a fair amount of pride in our sense of independence and self-reliance. The idea of calling another person to ask assistance in finding a job runs counter to our feelings of self-reliance and may at first seem degrading. There is also the added sense of humiliation experienced when the situation involves recent job loss as well.

As with fear of rejection, those who are embarrassed to ask others for help in their job search must quickly get beyond these feelings if they are to be successful. The answer lies in the networking method itself. If properly done, employment networking will allow you to carefully avoid placing the person contacted in an awkward or embarrassing position. It is a dignified process that allows others to help to the extent they are able but does not pressure them to do so.

So, there is no need for embarrassment. This fact will become clearer as you become more familiar and comfortable with the specifics of the networking process.

The "Indirect" Approach

The mistake most frequently made by the novice, untrained networker is to ask contacts *directly* for jobs or job leads. This direct approach places the contact on the spot and can cause a great deal of embarrassment and awkwardness if the contact is not able to respond in a meaningful way. When this happens, the contact wants to end the conversation and get off the phone.

Instead, what is needed is a softer, more "indirect" networking approach that allows the contact to more gracefully "get off the hook," if they are genuinely unable to assist you with your job search.

The problem with the direct approach (i.e., asking directly for jobs or job leads) is that most persons contacted by you may not be in a position to provide either immediately. You are asking them for something they are unable to deliver. The result is a sense of awkwardness and embarrassment that ends in an abbreviated phone conversation which produces little or no tangible assistance for your job search.

By contrast, effective networking is intentionally designed to be an indirect process. By this, I mean that one carefully avoids asking directly for jobs and/or job leads. Instead, the focus of effective networking is to ask the contact for *deliverables,* i.e., advice, counsel, contacts, things the contact can provide. By requesting the things that contacts can provide, a far more relaxed conversation ensues between the networker and the networking contact, with the high likelihood that the person contacted will automatically volunteer jobs and/or job leads (often without even being asked to do so).

When planning a networking call, you should establish objectives for the call prior to making it. Think, beforehand, about the kind of specific assistance the contact is most likely able to provide and then plan your call accordingly. Examples of the types of assistance that might be provided are:

1. Job hunting advice.
2. Information about target industries.
3. Information about target companies.
4. Names of key industry contacts.
5. Names of key professional contacts.
6. Job leads.

When placing a networking call, the call will normally be far more productive if you start with making "general" requests (i.e., advice about job hunting, information about target industries, information about target companies) and then work toward making the more "specific" requests (i.e., names of key industry contacts, names of key professional contacts) toward the end of the conversation. Reserve requests for job leads to the very later stages of your networking call. If you handle the call well, the likelihood is that your contact will automatically volunteer this information, and you will never have to request it.

Finally, by using this indirect, softer approach you will create the impression that you are a person who is sensitive and diplomatic—someone who can be trusted. The way you deal with these contacts suggests to them that you deal with others in the same way. If you are sensitive and diplomatic in your approach, there is a great likelihood you will deal with others in the same fashion. Such treatment makes your contacts feel more comfortable in sharing the names of some of their better, more valuable contacts. They know that you will respect these important referrals and will not embarrass them by behaving inappropriately.

So, there are several excellent reasons to utilize the indirect approach, and you will find it a *far* more productive approach than asking persons for jobs and/or job leads directly. Let's now examine the elements of an effective networking call.

Elements of a Good Networking Call

Years of observing hundreds of people making employment calls has led to the conclusion that there are certain basic elements that comprise an effective networking conversation. These are as follows:

1. Introduction.
2. Name and relationship of referral.
3. Small talk.
4. Statement—purpose of the call.
5. Short summary of employment qualifications (the two-minute drill).
6. General requests:
   a. Request for job hunting advice
   b. Request for information/advice about target industry
   c. Request for information/advice about target companies
7. Specific requests:
   a. Names of key industry contacts
   b. Names of key professional contacts
   c. Names of key personal contacts
   d. Permission to use name as a "referral"
8. Statement of appreciation.

Let's discuss these elements so you can see exactly how they can be employed to your advantage.

Introduction and Referral Statement

Usually an introduction includes a reference to the person who has made the referral. Including the name of the referral as part of the introduction is the thing that makes networking work. It creates the sense of "social obligation" that makes the contact feel a need to be responsive to your request for help.

The following are some sample introductory statements:

Good morning John. This is Alice Hartman calling. I am calling at the suggestion of Glen Peters, who seemed to feel you might be able to help me. Glen tells me that you are a person who is very knowledgeable of the paper industry and suggested that you might be a good person to speak with.

Hello, Darlene, I am a friend of David Dawson. In a recent conversation, Dave gave me your name as someone who is very active in the National Association of Marketing Professionals and who might be someone who could give me some ideas and advice.

In making the introduction, you will note that the name of the referral is used almost immediately in an effort to establish a personal connection with the person being called. You will also notice how the introduction is used to position the "indirect" approach. Note, for example, use of words such as *ideas, advice,* etc. in the second sample introductive statement.

Small Talk

The use of small talk, following the introduction, sets the stage for the discussion and establishes a more informal tone. This informal tone is conducive to a more relaxed, casual conversation that will likely yield the kind of information and assistance you are looking for than a more formal tone might yield.

Where appropriate, the introduction might be followed by some small talk. The following are some examples of the "small talk technique."

Dave tells me that the two of you have spent the last five years on the Association's Board and have enjoyed some interesting challenges together.

Mary says that you are an avid sailor and that the two of you have spent many an hour plying the waters of the Long Island Sound together. I understand that you won the Memorial Day race last year at the Moorings Yacht Club. Congratulations!

Examination of these sample small talk scenarios will show you how easy it is to create a more relaxed, casual tone to the networking conversation. It is a good idea to ask your original contact to describe the nature of his or her relationship with the person you will be calling as an additional strategy for maximizing the upcoming networking call. This frequently provides some excellent material for structuring the "small talk" strategy to use in the subsequent networking conversation.

Purpose of Call

Following the small talk, you will need to state the purpose of your call. This should be very brief and straightforward. Note how this statement makes use of the indirect approach as the basis for positioning your conversation. Specifically, you are *not* calling for a job or for job leads—you are calling for advice, information, etc. (the "deliverables").

Here are some ways to state the purpose of your call:

John, I am in the process of a career transition, and am calling you for some general advice and ideas. Sam seemed to think you might be a good person to talk with in this regard.

Carolyn, I have decided to leave my position as Controller of Warrington Corporation, and am calling you for some general advice and counsel concerning my job search. Bill felt you would be an excellent sounding board on this subject, and I would welcome your thoughts and ideas.

You can see how effectively the indirect approach can be applied at this juncture of the conversation. By stating that you are calling for advice, ideas, counsel, and the like, you have set the stage for a far more productive conversation and have placed your contact at ease by asking him or her for those things that they can deliver to you.

The Two-Minute Drill

After you have stated the purpose of your call, the usual response of the other party is to ask about your background and qualifications. It is at this point that you need to be prepared to deliver your *two-minute drill.*

The two-minute drill is nothing more than a short description (usually not more than two minutes in length) of your qualifications and interests. The following is a sample of a typical two-minute drill.

Ann, I am currently Vice President of Human Resources for Latril Corporation, a $600 million, 1,200 employee manufacturer of industrial specialty pumps sold to the chemical industry. Prior to this, I spent nearly 18 years in the paper industry with Champion International, where I advanced through a series of increasingly important human resources management positions including: Manager of Corporate Employment, Director of Human Resources for the Western Region, H.R. Manager for Corporate Staff, and, finally, Corporate Director of Human Resources. I moved to Latril Corporation, as Vice President, two years ago. I miss the East Coast and have therefore elected to make a job change. I would be interested in a senior level human resources position with a medium-to-large size company near any of the major metropolitan areas in the Northeast.

As you can see, the two-minute drill is short, sweet, and to the point. It provides just enough information about your qualifications and interests to allow the other person to be of assistance to you, but it does not bog them down with unnecessary detail. To prepare for the two-minute drill, it is a good idea to write it out on a $4'' \times 5''$ index card before beginning your networking calls. This will force you to be concise and to the point, providing only the relevant information needed by your contact.

General Requests

Following the two-minute drill, the next step in an effective networking strategy is to request general assistance from the person you have contacted. In doing this, you should be making effective use of the indirect approach by requesting advice, ideas, thoughts, guidance, counsel, and so forth. Here are some examples:

Sarah tells me that you are particularly knowledgeable of the steel industry and might be able to shed some light on some of the current industry trends that might impact my job search. I would really appreciate if you could share some of your knowledge and insight in this regard.

According to Ginger, you have had a lot of employment experience and would be a good person to talk with concerning my job search strategy. I would really welcome your ideas and suggestions.

As can be seen from these examples, the indirect approach is based upon the idea of asking your contact for "deliverables:" ideas, counsel, advice, and all things that the contact can and will almost always provide. Giving general advice will frequently "warm the person up" and get them thinking constructively about ways they can help you. Most will have several ideas and suggestions.

During this part of the conversation, a great deal of personal rapport is normally established. The personal relationship that is established here serves as an excellent basis for the introduction of the more specific kinds of requests.

Specific Requests

Having established a closer relationship as the result of the dialogue around your request for general information, it is now time to turn the conversation to requests for "specific" information (i.e., names of key contacts, job leads, etc.).

Here are some examples of how to request this kind of information:

According to Bill, you have been very active in the American Manufacturer's Association here in the Philadelphia area and might be in a position to help me identify some of the key Association members who, like yourself, are well-connected in the area's manufacturing community. I would really appreciate any thoughts you might have in this regard. Who are some of the people it would be good for me to talk with?

Nancy, as you think about some of the key personnel moves in the industry, like retirements, promotions, resignations, and so forth, are you aware of any possible openings for senior level financial executives?

Once you have been successful in acquiring the names of key industry or professional contacts from the person through whom you are networking, it is a good idea to request permission to use their name as a referral. Here is how that might be accomplished:

> Thanks for sharing Sam's name with me. Would you mind if I told him that you suggested I call?

This is important, since the power of employment networking is based upon the "social connectedness" between the person who has referred you and the party to whom you have been referred. It is the relationship between these two that creates the sense of social (or professional) obligation to respond to your request for assistance, and is the glue that keeps the networking process together. Acquiring the person's permission to use their name as a referral is thus very important to making the process work well.

Statement of Appreciation

The final element of the networking process is the *statement of appreciation*. This is nothing more than a simple "thank you" for the advice and assistance provided to you.

In those cases where a contact has been particularly helpful and appears to be well connected, it would be a good idea to write a letter expressing your appreciation and to include a copy of your resume as well.

Hopefully, this chapter has provided you with the means to prepare and execute a highly effective job-hunting campaign at the executive level. These well-proven techniques have helped numerous senior level executives to land attractive positions.

10

INTERVIEW PREPARATION

In recent years, employers have demonstrated steady and decided improvement in the thoroughness with which executive
employment interviews are conducted. Employers no longer
simply assume that because executive candidates have held
responsible positions with another firm that they will provide
successful leadership to the business unit for which they are
being recruited.

Instead, in today's business environment, most candidates
for key executive positions can expect a much more thorough
"grilling" and a far more thorough examination of both their
ability and motivation to perform the position for which they
are under consideration. In fact, with the advent and growing
use of behavior-based interviewing methods, executive candidates are now expected to provide "behavioral evidence" of
capability to perform critical elements of the position, rather
than simply stating that they are capable of such performance.
Candidates for executive level positions must prepare for the
interview process accordingly.

Consistent with the underlying theme of executive success,
this chapter will prepare the reader for the rigors of a behavior-
based interview that focuses on those areas, proven by our

survey, to be important to the success of the modern executive management candidate. It is these areas that can be expected to be probed with increased intensity as employers attempt to grapple with the need to fill key positions with highly capable and productive leaders.

DESIRE FOR IMPROVED EXECUTIVE STAFFING

It has become increasingly clear to most employers that the selection of executive leadership to fill key management positions within the organization cannot be left to chance. There is simply too much to lose. The new, emerging business climate characterized by leaner, flatter organizations and fierce global competition for market share leaves little alternative but to select those who have the qualifications and capacity to succeed in these key leadership roles.

In recent years, therefore, we are seeing the emergence of improved interview methods and techniques designed to "measure" executive capability. At the heart of this movement is the "behavior-based" interview, which is designed to use candidate behavior as the basis for predicting future job performance success.

Modern interview theory subscribes to the basic principle that "the greatest single predictor of future performance (behavior) is present or past performance (behavior) in the same or similar kinds of work." Hence, organizations are now beginning to better understand that if you are going to predict the probability of good performance in a key executive position, you must examine the candidate's present or past performance (behavior) in the same or similar kinds of work. As a result, modern executive interviews are designed to examine such behavior.

The Behavioral Interview

At the core of most behavior-based interview approaches is the use of either real or hypothetical situations requiring problem solving on the candidate's part. These are normally posed as scenarios, and the candidate is asked what he or she would do to address each situation. Usually, the scenario is carefully designed to replicate, as closely as possible, real problems that the candidate will face in the job itself. In this way, the employer can observe what the candidate will do (behavior) to address these problems. It is believed that how the candidate responds (behaves) during the interview will likely be a fairly reliable indicator of how the candidate will perform (behave) in the job itself.

The message here for the modern executive employment candidate is *be prepared for the behavior-based employment interview*. You must be prepared to demonstrate behavioral evidence of your capabilities. This chapter will help you to prepare for success in handling these behavior-based interview questions.

EMPLOYER INTERVIEW TARGET AREAS

The main theme of this book has been directed at what it takes to succeed as an executive in a changing and emerging business climate. This chapter is no different. It will focus on those areas that employers, in response to our survey, have indicated are most important to executive success in business today. Since these are the areas most valued by employers, it should be safe to conclude that they will be the main focal point of most executive interviews.

This chapter will systematically examine each of these key focus areas in an effort to better prepare executive employment candidates for the kinds of questions they can expect to encounter in the interview. Our approach will be to identify each of these key focal areas, to help the reader to anticipate the kinds of questions likely to be asked in each of these categories, and to suggest some interview strategies for successfully preparing to address each. In this way, the reader will be strategically prepared to address those areas most likely to be probed with some intensity by the employer, thereby substantially increasing the probability of successful interview results.

Leadership

As discussed in earlier chapters, the role of executive leadership is rapidly changing. Prior reliance on "top down" decision making as the executive leadership standard has given way to a new order. This new order is in keeping with the trend toward flatter organizations, with each executive having a much broader span of control (i.e., a far greater number of direct reports). Not surprisingly, successful executives can no longer make all the decisions and pass them down to subordinates for execution.

In order to lead effectively in such organizations, modern executives are expected to embrace a "participative" leadership style—one that is designed to get things done "through others" rather than to directly make all of the decisions themselves. Hence, in the interview, employers will be looking for behavioral evidence of such "participative" leadership style. The following (or similar) direct questions are thus likely to find their way into the employer's interview design, and you will need to be prepared to answer them:

1. Can you describe your management style?
2. How would you characterize your management philosophy?
3. How would your subordinates categorize your management style?
   a. What would they say they like about how you manage?
   b. What improvements would they likely suggest?

In contrast to these *direct* questions, here are some examples of *behavior-based* interview questions designed to probe your leadership philosophy and style. Note how these questions are designed to examine how you go about managing others (i.e., your management behavior).

1. Describe your overall planning process.
   a. How do you go about establishing both long- and short-term objectives?

b. What is the process you use to develop both long- and short-term plans?

2. How are decisions made when it is necessary to allocate scarce resources (i.e., capital, people, etc.) between various parts of your organization?

3. In times of major crisis, how are issues resolved within your organization?

4. What are the two or three key things that are most important to your organization's success? Why are these important?

As you can see, these behavior-based interview questions are constructed to allow the employer to observe how you behave as a manager. They are designed to collect *behavioral evidence* that you are (or are not) a participative manager, by determining the degree to which you involve your employees in management decision-making processes. Where an executive candidate describes *no* subordinate involvement in either key planning or decision making, there appears to be good behavioral evidence that this executive is *not* a proponent of participative management. Most modern organizations will quickly screen such candidates out and continue with their employment search for those who better align with the socio-technical systems approach to management.

Thus, from an interview strategy standpoint, it is important for you to understand that most employers will be looking for some reasonable level of employee involvement and participation when describing your management planning and decision-making processes. In the absence of such involvement, the assumption is that you are an old-fashioned, controllive-style manager who makes most of the decisions her- or himself and does little to get employee involvement and ownership in the key decisions that are made. Our survey clearly substantiates that this is not the style of management believed important to executive success in today's business culture.

The data from our executive success survey suggests that the preferred leadership style sought by most organizations is that of the "participative" leader. This individual is generally described as one who provides vision and direction and is then able to tap and fully utilize the capability of the organization's human resources through extensive employee involvement in the decision-making processes. Such individuals are generally described as those who enjoy "getting results through others" rather that those who enjoy the management of "things." Other words used to describe this preferred management style are *coach, teacher, counselor, enabler, cheerleader,* etc.

Well-informed executive candidates will do well to pay keen attention to our survey data if they are to successfully prepare for the modern executive employment interview. Whether asked to describe their management style, philosophy, planning and/or business decision-making processes, they will want to be sure to include indications of a heavy dose of employee involvement and participation and to describe their management leadership role as that of counselor, coach, teacher, enabler, and the like.

Our survey of executive success suggests that a second dimension of leadership that corporations believe important to executive effectiveness is the area of *interpersonal skills.* The increasing internal complexity of organizations coupled with the need for building more effective relationships with customers (both internal and external) requires executives to develop strong interpersonal skills. They must deal effectively with a broader range and ever-increasing array of individuals both within and outside their organization. As a result, interpersonal skills (i.e., the ability to relate effectively to a wide range of individuals) is taking on ever-increasing importance as a selection criteria in the hiring of executive level talent. Thus, employers are placing increasing importance on probing this area during the course of the employment interview.

The following are typical questions that executive candidates can expect to encounter as a means of gauging the strength of their interpersonal skills:

1. With what kind of people do you most enjoy working? Why?

2. With what kind of people do you least like working? Why?

3. How would you describe your relationship with your current boss?
   a. In what ways do you most agree? Why?
   b. In what areas do you least agree? Why?
   c. How do you manage your disagreements?
4. In your current position, with whom do you enjoy the
   closest relationship? Why?
5. With whom are you least comfortable?
   a. Why?
   b. What do you do to resolve these differences?
6. Of your past bosses, with whom were you least
   comfortable?
   a. In what ways were you least compatible?
   b. How did you deal with your differences?

As you can see, these questions are designed to focus on
areas of disagreement or incompatibility. How these questions
are answered will certainly provide employers with strong evidence of your interpersonal effectiveness.

When employing these kinds of questions as the basis for
assessing interpersonal skills, employers are looking for the
following:

1. Evidence of compatibility (or incompatibility) with others (especially reoccurring patterns).
2. Ability (or inability) to effectively manage and resolve
   interpersonal conflict.
3. Openness (or resistance) to the ideas and views of others.
4. Flexibility (or rigidity) of approach.
5. Warmth, friendliness, approachability, charisma.

Good performance in the employment interview will require
executive employment candidates to demonstrate strong interpersonal skills. Guidelines for accomplishing this are:

1. Avoid describing incompatible relationships (with bosses,
   peers, or subordinates).

2. If "forced" to describe a less than perfect relationship, cite one that was not particularly serious and where you were successful in patching things up.

3. Indicate a general openness and willingness to consider the ideas of others even when these ideas are very different from your own.

4. Be prepared to demonstrate ways in which you have been resourceful, creative, and flexible when dealing with others having an opposite viewpoint from your own.

5. Indicate that you believe encouraging diverse viewpoints is critical to the health and well-being of the organization. Only by constantly challenging the status quo can the organization develop an environment that embraces continuous improvement.

Related to this area of interpersonal skills is the matter of diversity. Our survey data shows that modern organizations prefer executive leadership styles that value diversity of viewpoints and executive demonstrations of ability to draw from different viewpoints represented in a group. These data suggest that modern organizations actively seek those executives who see organizational richness in the variety of cultures and viewpoints represented in a diverse employee base. Successful executives seek to harness the power of these diverse views in the form of new, creative ideas and solutions that provide a competitive advantage for the organization. Clearly, the modern executive leader is expected to actively nurture diversity of viewpoint and to provide a work environment where all persons can contribute their ideas and viewpoints freely, without threat from others.

It is important to interview effectiveness, therefore, that candidates for executive positions proclaim their commitment to employee diversity and voice commitment to the free expression of ideas as important means to assuring continuous improvement and competitive superiority.

The following are some examples of interview questions that may be used by employers to measure the commitment of executive candidates to employee diversity:

1. What techniques do you use to resolve strong differences of opinion between two or more employees?

2. What do you do when two or more employees are in strong opposition to a decision made by the majority of their fellow workers? How do you manage this?

3. In your judgment, is it more important to encourage diverse thinking in your group or to create a harmonious team that is in total agreement? Why?

4. Which type of organization, in your opinion, has the greatest potential for ultimate success?
   a. A team comprised of individuals with dramatically different viewpoints on key issues?
   b. A team comprised of individuals with substantially similar viewpoints on key issues? Why?

In each of the foregoing questions, interview success will require you to emphasize the value of diversity. Organizations are increasingly coming to understand and appreciate the importance of diversity of individual thought and ideas to the overall health and long-range success of the organization.

Organizations that are rich in ideas and viewpoint are clearly at a competitive long-range advantage. It is believed that it is from the richness in the differences of ideas and viewpoints that new, creative ways are found that are better and provide the organization with the ability to distinguish itself from competition in the marketplace. Singularity of thought may sometimes win in the short-run, but in the long-run it is always the advent of creative, innovative ideas that brings about meaningful change and long-term progress.

PRODUCTIVITY

As we already know from previous discussion, organizations are increasingly assigning a premium to those executives who get results. The new order requires executives to do more faster, better, with less. Flatter organizations with reduced resources require executives who have the ability and know-how to increase output and improve quality, despite dwindling resources (i.e., capital, people, raw materials, etc.).

As part of this new emphasis on productivity, our survey data indicates that problem solvers are "in." Organizations value those who get results. The need to do more with less requires the "complete" executive—one who can define the problems, develop the appropriate strategies and lead others in implementing successful solutions. Those who are simply "implementers" are of less value to the modern organization, while those who are only "strategists" are of little value as well.

This need for increased effectiveness and productivity is set against a backdrop of increasing complexity and uncertainty. The unprecedented rate of change faced by most organizations requires executive talent capable of effectively coping with an increased level of ambiguity and uncertainty and the ability to maintain a high level of discipline and focus. Further, to meet critical deadlines within increasingly shorter time frames, corporations are seeking those who can effectively manage and apply the most recent technology designed to enhance their overall effectiveness and productivity.

All of this has resulted in an increased level of demand for executives who have a track record for getting results. The new, emerging culture is highly focused on efficiency and results, and executive employment interviews are now beginning to focus more and more on the candidate's ability to achieve organizational objectives, despite decreased time frames and ever-decreasing resources.

In preparing for a successful interview, therefore, executives need to focus their attention on the results they have achieved and their ability to respond quickly (and meaningfully) to new challenges. Of particular importance is the ability to apply technology in achieving a higher level of results faster. This normally translates into the ability to apply the latest functional methods and management processes, much of which relies on computer-based technology.

A valuable approach to use when preparing for this aspect of the executive employment interview is to perform a thorough, systematic analysis of the positions you have held. Here is a guideline that should help facilitate this process:

1. What were principal functions for which you were accountable?
2. What were the goals and results expected of you in each of these key functional areas?
3. What were the key challenges and problems that you had to resolve to achieve these results?
4. What did you do to solve these problems?
5. What were the results that you achieved (measured in quantitative terms)?

When citing examples of your productivity, make sure to select specific accomplishments where you were responsible for defining the problem, developing the strategy, and implementing the results. Avoid selecting those in which you either simply performed the analysis or implemented the solution only. Remember, modern organizations are seeking leaders who are capable of doing all three—those who are able to solve key problems and add meaningful value in pursuit of the organization's vision and goals.

When facing a skillful interviewer who is intent on probing your overall productivity as an executive, here are some interview questions you are likely to encounter:

1. Describe the key functional accountabilities of your current position.
2. Which of these is most important to job success? Why?
3. What have been the toughest problems you have had to face in meeting these accountabilities?
4. How did you tackle these problems?
5. Specifically, what did you do, and what were the results?
6. Could these results have been improved? How?

7. What would you now do differently to achieve an improved level of result?

8. What was your role (versus the role of others) in achieving these key results?

9. What new knowledge, skills, and abilities might have improved your ability to achieve even better results in these important areas in the future?

10. In solving these problems, what were the principal uncertainties and ambiguities with which you were faced? How did you manage these?

11. In solving the "X" problem, were there other approaches you might have used?
    a. What were they?
    b. Why did you choose the approach that you did?
    c. Would you use this particular approach again? Why?

As can be readily seen from the above sample interview questions, successful interviewing requires a good deal of advanced preparation on the part of the executive candidate. The questions cited here, however, should prepare you to answer the "productivity" related questions you will encounter. In preparing for your interview, therefore, it would be a good idea to walk back through your last several managerial assignments, applying this set of questions to each position held. In doing so, you will be well-prepared to cite several specific examples of accomplishments and results (along with quantitative measurements), which will show you as an executive who is strongly committed to achieving results and bringing continuous improvement to the organization.

Where possible, it will greatly enhance your interview effectiveness if you select specific results that were accomplished despite significantly reduced resources (i.e., reduced budgets, decreased staffing, etc.). Additionally, examples chosen (where possible) should reflect extremely tight deadlines coupled with limited resources. Such examples best fit the executive selection standard of doing more better with less, a standard that is becoming increasingly valued by most companies.

QUALITY

Our survey data clearly support the fact that there is an unprecedented quality revolution taking place in American industry today. Forced by increasing domestic and global competition that has in many cases threatened their very survival, many corporations during the late 1980s and early 1990s have plunged headlong into major quality improvement efforts. At the core of this revolution is Dr. W. Edwards Deming's 14 points for management and the SPC-based "total quality" approaches now promoted by many of the world's Total Quality gurus.

Our survey highlights the fact that the quality factor has found itself on the "front page" as an important prerequisite to executive career success. It thus has became a major qualification sought by most organizations when filling executive leadership positions.

According to feedback provided through our survey of leading corporations and business schools, there are several quality-related dimensions required to succeed in the executive role in today's business climate. As suggested earlier in this book, they include:

1. Strong commitment to achieving quality results.
2. Possessing a "customer-driven focus."
3. Ability to shift employee focus from merely "satisfying" the customer to "anticipating" customer wants.
4. Desire to "quantify" results—requiring measurable proof that "it works."
5. Insistence on measurable standards in previously "nonquantifiable" areas.

Because of the increasing importance of the total quality movement in American industry today, executives can fully expect to encounter interview questions directed at their understanding of, and commitment to, the underlying principles of the total quality concept. Prospective employers are more and more wanting to know whether or not executive candidates understand these fundamental principles, and whether they are adept at applying them to the functional areas they manage.

Today's modern executive is expected to fully embrace the belief that all work design and processes need to be customer-focused. Whether that customer is external (the ultimate consumer of the organization's products or services) or internal (someone to whom goods or services are provided within the organization), the sole purpose for the existence of the business function for which the executive is responsible is to satisfy the customer. Therefore, all work must be focused to that end.

Increasingly so, leading employers are measuring customer satisfaction in measurable, statistical terms. They work closely in partnership with their customers (both internal and external) to qualitatively and quantitatively study those factors critical to customer satisfaction as a means to improving both their products and processes.

In some organizations, it is not enough to simply satisfy the customer's *current* needs. Instead, the focus is now on anticipating the *future* needs of the customer and seeking to establish the measurable standards required to satisfy these future requirements as well.

Once these customer-focused quality standards have been established, they drive right back into the executive's own shop, where all aspects of the work process are examined (using statistical techniques) to determine which factors most impact customer satisfaction. Through such reengineering efforts, necessary changes and improvements are then made to the way work is done to assure 100 percent satisfaction.

Organizations have come to appreciate the competitive and economic advantage of the total quality approach. The benefits of "doing it right the first time" are several. Some are:

1. A totally satisfied customer, translating into continuous repeat business.

2. A competitive market advantage (hard for competition to dislodge you).

3. Higher profits:
    a. No product returns from customers.
    b. No need for a customer service department to handle customer complaints.
    c. No need to incur the cost of disposal of returned product.
    d. No waste of raw materials.
    e. Lower raw material inventory levels.
    f. Smaller, more efficient work force.

The list of benefits to be realized by the organization from total quality and reengineering initiatives is practically endless. It is for this reason that many hiring organizations are now paying keen attention to an executive's qualifications in this important arena when selecting top leadership.

The following questions are representative of the interview questions that executive candidates might expect to encounter during today's interview, as employers attempt to assess their commitment to (and proficiency in) achieving the customer-driven goals associated with total quality and reengineering efforts.

1. What criteria do you feel are most important in gauging the success at any organization you manage? How do you measure this success?

2. What are currently the two or three most important goals you have established for the organization you manage?

3. What standards have been established to measure the progress of your organizational unit?

4. Whom do you consider to be your organization's primary customer(s)? How do you measure customer satisfaction?

5. What key criteria are used to reward employee and/or group performance in your organization? How is performance measured against these criteria?

As you can see, the above interview questions are very effective vehicles for probing an executive's qualifications in the quality area. Answers to these and similar questions will quickly flush out those executives who do not measure up in this important leadership area. Those who do not demonstrate a customer-driven focus and who fail to show an appreciation for quantitative measurement of results will go by the wayside quickly in favor of these who do.

In preparing for the interview, therefore, your success will often depend heavily on how well-prepared you are to effectively answer these quality-related questions. It is certainly clear from our survey data that corporations are now placing a decided premium on those executives who fully embrace the customer-driven, total quality principles of management.

VISION

Our survey has solidly established the ability to be *visionary* as a valued attribute sought in today's executive management candidate. As discussed earlier, it is the executive's vision that provides the overall direction and focus required for organizational success. We can expect, therefore, to see this as an area for focus during the executive interview.

Generally, in the "current" context, vision means having the ability to see the big picture and the relationship (as well as integration) of all of the parts. It also embodies a "future" notion, suggesting the ability to look out into the future and forecast (and plan for) key events that will impact the success of an enterprise. Persons with vision have the unique ability to picture a desired future state, which then becomes the basis for both establishing goals and planning most effective use of the organization's resources.

The ability to be visionary is taking on added importance with the rapid advance of global competition and the increased competitive intensity now being felt by most organizations at the domestic level. Executives who are able to see the big picture in the context of an ever-changing marketplace and understand the key shifts required to position their organization to win are a hot commodity in today's executive marketplace.

When assessing executive vision during the employment interview, employers will frequently focus on the candidate's ability to think strategically. The following represent common interview questions designed to explore this area:

1. What are the two or three most difficult external issues which threaten the success of your organization?

2. What strategies and plans have you developed to address these?

3. What other options did you consider when formulating your current strategy? Why?

4. What factors most influenced selection of your current strategy?

5. What do you foresee as the outcome of your current strategy? Why?

6. As you look out into the future, what long-term changes will likely be required for future success? Why?

7. In what ways are you planning for these now?

8. What are the two or three major internal problems that most threaten the success of your organization?

9. What plans and strategies have you put into place to address these? Why?

10. What are other possible solutions? Why did you not elect to pursue these?

Successful executive job seekers will need to be able to effectively field these and similar questions, if they are going to exhibit the vision and foresight that modern organizations value and seek in their executive talent. Clearly, careful thought on how to best answer these questions will go a long way toward helping executive employment candidates to be victorious in the employment interview. Managers who do not exhibit the vision, creativity, and broad strategic thinking skills prized by organizations will quickly fall by the wayside in favor of those possessing these important attributes.

FUNCTIONAL EXPERTISE

Our survey on executive career success supports the fact that organizations place a great deal of emphasis on functional expertise as a criteria for executive selection. Survey results show that organizations prefer executives who continue to grow and develop their knowledge in their field of specialty. Such functional competence is heavily relied on in formulating key business decisions and in deciding important business matters.

In today's ever-changing business climate, organizations cite a decided preference for those executives who are committed to a process of continuous personal improvement and development. Rapidly changing technology and intensification of competitive pressure in the marketplace require leaders who stay abreast in their field through education and personal development.

Our survey data shows that successful executives have two common attributes when it comes to personal development:

1. Intellectual curiosity and thirst for knowledge.
2. Recognition that learning is a life-long process for everyone.

Although functional expertise has always been a major focus area for executive evaluation and selection, there appears to be an increased emphasis on the need to remain current in one's field. Due in most part to the information explosion, the rate at which change is occurring in recent years has accelerated rapidly. As change continues to occur, it is beginning to occur at an ever-increasing rate of speed. Functional obsolescence is thus becoming an increasing reality among those executives not committed to personal development.

As successful organizations focus more and more on strategies required to meet and beat competition in the marketplace, the need for continuous management development is taking on increased emphasis. In order to beat competition, it is necessary to staff key executive positions with smarter, more capable individuals. Such individuals have the ability to do more, faster, and better, thus providing the competitive advantage needed to win.

When exploring functional expertise, the following interview questions are typical of those likely to be asked of executive employment candidates. Being prepared to address these questions with intelligent answers will facilitate executive interview success.

1. What do you believe to be the two or three most significant developments in your field in the last two years?

2. What do you feel is the significance of these developments? Why are they important?

3. What, in your opinion, are the hallmarks for professional excellence (the state-of-the-art so to speak) in your functional area of expertise?

4. How does the function you manage measure up to these standards?

5. In what areas do you meet or exceed these standards?

6. In what areas is there room for improvement? Why?

7. What is your strategy for developing a world-class function?

8. What things do you do to remain current and up-to-date in your field?

9. On a scale of 1 to 10, where would you rate your overall knowledge and expertise in your field? Why?

10. In what areas do you most need to develop and improve to be current in your field?

11. What is your plan to achieve this improvement?

In addition to these fairly direct questions about functional knowledge and expertise, it is not at all uncommon for employers to employ situational interview questions when attempting to determine level of functional expertise in a given area. In using this approach, the employer will cite a particular situation or problem and then ask the executive candidate what he or she would do. Using such behavioral interview techniques allows the organization to observe whether or not the candidate has the requisite knowledge to successfully address the problem.

Usually the situations chosen as the basis for such interview questions are selected because of their technical complexity and their application of state-of-the-art functional know-how in arriving at the solution. Thus, the employer can determine not only whether the employment candidate has the required knowledge to solve the problem but also whether he or she can successfully apply this knowledge and arrive at a successful result.

This type of situational interview approach is growing in both popularity and use. Unfortunately, however, there is little the executive employment candidate can do in advance to anticipate and prepare for such interview questions.

PERSONAL CHARACTER

Finally, a characteristic important to executive career success is that of personal character. Our survey has shown that most organizations cite personal character as an area of great importance to success at the executive level. Apparently, such traits as openness, honesty, loyalty, and integrity are seen as important executive attributes in the executive suites of corporate America, and corporations clearly prefer candidates who demonstrate these virtues.

The *situational interview* is perhaps the most common interview technique used to gauge executive character. Usually, the situations posed to the candidate when using this approach require choices that have strong ethical overtones. Examples of such situational interview questions are as follows:

1. Would you prefer to be viewed as a winner or a person of high principles? Why?

2. If you had the opportunity to land a big order with an important customer but could only do so by delivering out-of-spec material (which the customer would likely not notice), what would you do?

3. If you discovered that your top salesperson, who is responsible for nearly 35 percent of your sales volume, was intentionally lying to customers to get large orders, how would you handle the matter?

4. If you discovered that a customer had been accidentally overcharged on an order some six months after having received payment, and it was highly unlikely that the customer would ever discover the error, what would you do? Why?

11

WINNING INTERVIEW STRATEGIES

In the preceding chapter, our focus was on the kinds of questions most likely to be asked of the executive employment candidate during the course of an interview. These questions, based on our executive success survey, focus on certain target areas identified as important to executive success. Obviously, being well-prepared to answer these questions is an important factor in planning a winning interview strategy. To prepare to successfully compete with other outstanding candidates, however, you will need to go a step beyond this.

Considering the high levels of compensation paid to many corporate executives, organizations clearly expect a corresponding return on their investment. Thus, most executive interviews will focus on the value that will be contributed by the executive in return for this investment. Consequently, executive candidates must be well-prepared to clearly articulate their value and uniqueness if they are to successfully compete in this intensely competitive arena. Establishing this sense of value and distinguishing yourself from the "herd" is the subject of this chapter.

THE GREAT MISTAKE

The single greatest mistake that many executives make in the employment interview, from a strategic standpoint, is to spend entirely too much time talking about qualifications that are of little interest to the employer. Avoiding this usually requires the executive to invest a little time at the beginning of the interview discussion to find out what it is the host is most interested to know. This ensures far more efficient use of interview time and substantially improves the probability of a favorable outcome.

Unfortunately, however, many executive employment candidates make the mistake of not determining the employer's primary interest areas. Consequently, they may drone on for hours about their skills and capabilities without the slightest clue whether or not these subject areas are of importance to the person with whom they are interviewing. Although this may not always be a fatal mistake, it is certainly not an approach that will enhance the chances of receiving an employment offer. Serious executives will not leave this matter to chance.

QUALIFYING THE EMPLOYER

If serious about substantially improving interview odds, the executive interviewee will do well to adapt the same strategy that has long helped top sales producers consistently achieve success. This strategy is known as *qualifying the buyer*. Successful sales strategists have long known that selling is strictly a hit-or-miss proposition, unless one has advance knowledge of those factors that will most influence the potential customer to buy the product. Without such foreknowledge, however, you are simply shooting in the dark.

We have all experienced the sales presentation where the salesperson rambles on and on indefinitely about the many fine attributes of the product without once stopping to determine what aspects of the product are important to us and would motivate us to buy. Unfortunately, despite an otherwise excellent sales presentation, such unfocused sales approaches seldom result in consummation of the sale.

Successful interviewees, like successful salespersons, realize the importance of qualifying the buyer right from the start of the employment discussion. If an employment offer is to be forthcoming, a random approach to discovering the employer's preferences is unlikely to yield the desired result.

It is important to interview success, therefore, that the executive candidate establish what is important to the employer right from the onset of the interview discussion. In this way, he or she can focus much of their discussion on those factors most critical to the employer's decision, thus stacking the deck in the interviewee's favor. The balance of this chapter presents several strategies for use in qualifying the employer and can provide the executive with a decided competitive advantage over others who are less skilled at the interview process.

IDEAL CANDIDATE STRATEGY

Although seldom used, the *ideal candidate strategy* is perhaps the most effective of all the interview strategies that have been applied by successful employment candidates. When utilizing this strategy, the executive candidate simply asks the employer to describe the "ideal candidate" for the position. The following are some different approaches for implementing this strategy:

John, as you think about the overall requirements and challenges of this position, what criteria do you feel will be most important to successful performance?

Linda, if you think about the ideal candidate for this position, what overall qualifications, traits, and characteristics quickly come to mind? Why are these important?

Sam, in your judgment, what kind of person is ideally suited for this position?

Judy, how would you describe the ideal candidate for this position? What factors are really important to you?

By applying this strategy, you can gain a significant competitive advantage. Answers to these questions will tell you exactly what the hiring manager is looking for and thus allow you to focus discussion on those selection criteria most important to that employer's decision. These are the very areas most likely to impact the employer's decision.

By using the ideal candidate strategy early in the interview discussion, you improve your chances considerably. Such advance determination of important selection criteria allows you the balance of the interview to "package" yourself as the perfect candidate for the position. It will clearly provide a competitive advantage over other candidates who fail to determine the employer's selection preferences.

PERFORMANCE IMPROVEMENT STRATEGY

We have talked in previous chapters about the importance of improved productivity as a key factor in executive success. Our executive success survey has shown this to be an important element to executive success in today's business climate.

This "productivity" orientation by employers is the basis for our next interview strategy, the "performance opportunity" strategy. The focus of this strategy is to determine what areas of the job need to be better performed—hence the name *performance improvement* strategy.

The following are some questions that can be used by the executive candidate to effectively apply this interview strategy:

1. In your opinion, what aspects of this position could be better performed? And, what kind of improvement would you like to see?

2. What kinds of performance improvement would you most like to see in this position? Why?

3. What, in your judgment, are the key improvement opportunities for this position?

4. What three or four major improvements would you most like to see brought to this position?

5. To be considered "highly successful" in this position, what three or four things will a person need to accomplish over the next year or so? Why are these important to you?

6. If it were two years from now, what kinds of things would you expect to see in place in this position that are not in place now?

As you can see, the thrust of this interview strategy is productivity improvement. By simply asking these kinds of questions, the executive candidate automatically conveys the image of someone who is focused on bringing about efficiency and productivity improvement. By citing things that can be done to bring about improvement in the desired areas, the candidate further cements him- or herself as a preferred candidate for the position.

Key to the success of this interview strategy is that it serves to further qualify the employer. By having the employer identify specific areas in which improvement is desired, this strategy allows you the advantage of positioning yourself as someone who is well equipped to meet these particular challenges. By demonstrating your ability to add value in these important areas, you further enhance your competitive advantage over those whose interview approaches lack such employer focus.

As with the "ideal candidate," it is best to employ the "performance improvement" strategy toward the beginning of the interview discussion. In this way, you will build in sufficient time to allow yourself to effectively respond to the employer's stated performance improvement needs and thereby position yourself as a strong candidate who is able to bring these improvements to full actualization.

KEY PROBLEMS/CHALLENGES STRATEGY

As stated earlier in this book, "Problem solvers are in." Organizations are seeking executives who are capable of getting results—i.e., defining the problems, developing the strategy, and implementing the solution. Executives who are implementers or strategists only are considered far less valuable in the modern, down-sized corporate environment. Simply stated, companies are looking to hire "those who get results."

This growing demand for problem solvers coupled with the value modern organizations place on functional expertise, likely account for the success of the *key problems/challenges* interview strategy.

Related to the performance improvement strategy, but with a slightly different twist, the key problems (or challenges) interview strategy can prove a very effective technique. Instead of focusing on specific performance improvements, this strategy has as its main focus the major problems (or challenges) faced by the prospective employer.

The following questions are suggested for your use as a means of effectively employing this interview strategy:

1. What are the key problems you expect a successful candidate for this position to solve?

2. In your judgment, what are the two or three most critical challenges to be faced by this position?

3. What are the three or four most important problem areas that need to be addressed by this position?

4. What do you consider to be the most important challenges of this position? Why?

It is evident that the main reason why persons are hired and paid by corporations is their ability to solve problems. Without the need to solve problems there would be no jobs. Most compensation systems recognize this fact by providing higher levels of employee compensation for those required to solve the more complex and difficult problems. Conversely, positions requiring solution to only the simplest problems are generally those that are also the lowest paying.

The key problems/challenges strategy has the advantage of identifying those specific problems that the hiring manager (the one who will hire you) considers most important to job performance success. This strategy helps to further qualify the employer and provides you with the opportunity to position yourself as someone who has the ability to solve these critical problems.

Executive employment candidates who fail to clarify the employer's priorities in this important selection area will be at a decided disadvantage over those who do. It is important, therefore, that you identify these key problem areas early in the employment interview and proceed to position yourself as someone possessing the ability and motivation to effectively solve these problems and as someone who can bring improved performance and added value to the organization.

It is important to point out that the emphasis of this interview strategy is on what is important from the *employer's* standpoint, not from the candidate's point of view. Demonstrating the ability to solve problems in which the employer has no interest does little to enhance the employer's interest in you. Conversely, demonstrating ability to solve those key problems with which the employer is currently struggling is bound to raise considerable interest in bringing you aboard.

STRATEGIC CHANGE STRATEGY

A final interview strategy offering the potential for competitive advantage is the *strategic change* strategy. This approach, as suggested by our executive success survey data, should have great appeal to modern organizations seeking executives with vision and a desire for continuous improvement. Use of this strategy focuses on both and should serve to enhance your employment candidacy.

Most employment interviews tend to focus primarily on the "current position" rather than on the future. Thus, much of

the interview discussion is centered around the current problems and the current challenges of the position.

By contrast, the strategic change interview strategy gets
the employer thinking about the future. It highlights those
changes that must be brought about in order to achieve the
long-term, strategic goals of the organization. The following
are guideline questions that can be utilized to implement this
strategy:

1. As you think about the longer-term goals of the company,
   what key changes must this position initiate to support
   these goals?

2. What are some of the strategic, longer-term goals of this
   position? What key strategic changes must this position
   bring about?

3. What important changes must this position drive in
   order to support the organization's long-term strategic
   goals?
   a. What new problems will need to be solved?
   b. What new knowledge and skills will be needed for
      successful job performance?

4. What are some of the major areas of improvement
   needed by this position to support the organization's
   long term strategy?

Organizations that value executive vision will be on the
lookout for those candidates having a more strategic focus.
Asking about your responsibility for bringing about strategic
change is one way to telegraph to prospective employers that
you are someone who has the broader picture in mind. As
such, you will likely also be seen as one who values and pursues continuous improvement. Both of these characteristics
have been highlighted by our executive success survey as important for an executive candidate to succeed in today's business environment.

Few employment candidates ask strategically focused
questions of this sort. Most, by contrast, simply focus on the

position "as it now exists," leaving the impression that they are short-term, operations-oriented rather than strategically focused.

Through use of the strategic change strategy suggested here, you have an excellent opportunity to distinguish yourself from the multitudes and demonstrate that you have the vision required to successfully lead a major component of the organization. Needless to say, your candidacy will offer a sharp contrast to those who focus on only the short-term operational issues.

It should be clear from reading this chapter that there is a lot you can do from a strategy standpoint to favorably affect the outcome of the executive employment interview. Some practice with the strategies explained in this chapter should help put you in a far more powerful position and greatly improve your overall competitive position in the employment interview. Many whom we have personally counseled in the use of these techniques have returned from the toughest of employment interviews filled with excitement and a sense of tremendous success. Clearly, these are winning interview strategies that will serve you well, if you use them to your advantage.

12

CONCLUSION

In the last eleven chapters, we have come a long way in creating an understanding of the major shifts and changes taking place in the current business environment. These changes have been most significant and have had major consequences for executive career planning and job search. It is clear, if you are to succeed as executive, you must be willing to adjust to this changing environment and align your personal values and leadership style to the new, emerging culture. Without such adaptation, obsolescence and failure are all but guaranteed.

Our surveys have clearly demonstrated that today's successful executive is one who embraces change, values and encourages diverse viewpoints, continually challenges the status quo in search of something better, pursues excellence and continuous improvement, and is driven by the need to meet and exceed the expectations of customers at all times. The effective executive is also one who has a strong moral compass, is guided by high ideals and ethical standards, operates with a sense of fairness and integrity, is open, honest, and engenders a high level of trust, confidence, and respect in others.

Additionally, our findings show that the successful modern executive is one who has a global perspective, creates and communicates the vision of what is possible and desirable, provides strategic direction and focus, assures development of practical and workable plans, and motivates and encourages others to achieve the vision. Management style is highly participative, with a strong desire to achieve results through others. The successful executives prefer to manage processes rather than people, and sees his or her principal role as that of teacher, coach, facilitator—an enabler of others.

Further, the successful executive of today is driven to achieve ever-increasing levels of productivity improvement. He or she is able to increase output with reduced input, and is the embodiment of the success absolute—do more, faster, better, and with less.

As confirmed by our data, this is the yardstick of executive success by which aspiring executives are now being measured in the new, emerging business culture.

It is, therefore, the vision that should guide both career planning and personal development. And it is the achievement of this vision that should be the worthy goal of all those who seriously dream of reaching significant leadership positions in the new corporate America.

As a means to achieving this goal, executives need to be skilled at all aspects of job-hunting methodology. This is seen as an essential life skill that needs to be finely tuned and "at the ready" at all times. Whether as protection against the ever-present threat of job elimination or as a means to achieving new opportunities within the same firm, the executive must be able to successfully market him- or herself against ever-increasing competition.

It is clear, in the new business climate, that the old, tangible measurements of success (e.g., title, position, level, compensation) can no longer serve as the measuring sticks of success today. These are the artifacts of a past generation, when career success was principally measured via these hollow, external symbols. These visible badges of success are for the most part gone, and the new organization is now focused on equating career success with organizational success. In the mind of the modern organization, these two successes are endlessly entwined.

Today's executive success has taken on a far more intrinsic focus. Instead of striving for recognition through continuous promotion, each executive must now measure success from the standpoint of bringing value and continuous improvement to the organization. This is now the hallmark of executive effectiveness and the principal source of internal motivation and career satisfaction in the new business climate.

ENDNOTES

Chapter 1

1. Vincent P. Barabba, *Meeting of the minds: Creating the market-based enterprise* (Boston, MA: Harvard Business School Press, 1995) pp. 45, 46.

2. Steven Rayner "Making Employee Empowerment Work," *The Instant Access Guide to World Class Manufacturing* (Essex Junction, VT: Oliver Wight Publishing, Inc., 1994) pp. 153–154.

3. Daniel Tobin, "New Roles for Middle Managers," *The Omneo Edge,* April 1994, p. 2.

4. Unpublished, from an interview with Richard Luecke, April 1994.

5. John A. Byrne, "The Horizontal Organization," *Business Week,* December 20, 1993, pp. 76–81.

6. Walter Kiechel III, "A Manager's Career in the New Economy," *Fortune,* April 4, 1994, p. 70.

7. James M. Utterback, *Mastering the dynamics of innovation* (Boston, MA: Harvard Business School Press, 1994) p. xiv.

8. Robert Howard, "The CEO as Organizational Architect: An Interview with Xerox's Paul Allaire," *Harvard Business Review,* September–October 1992, p. 143.

9. Lee Dyer and Donna Blancero, "Workplace 2000," Working Paper 92-10, Center for Advanced Human Resources Studies, Cornell University, February 1992.

10. Charles Handy, *The age of unreason* (Boston, MA: Harvard Business School Press, 1989) p. 90.

Chapter 2

1. T. George Harris, "The Post-Capitalist Executive: An Interview with Peter F. Drucker," *Harvard Business Review,* May–June 1993, p. 117.

2. Richard Luecke, *Scuttle your ships before advancing: And other lessons from history on leadership and change for today's managers* (New York: Oxford University Press, 1994) p. 81.

3. Tom Peters, "50 Survival Strategies," *TPG Communications,* p. 4.

4. Peter F. Drucker, "The Coming of the New Organization," *Harvard Business Review,* January–February 1988, p. 45.

5. Michael T. Jacobs, *Short term America: The causes and cures of our business myopia* (Boston, MA: Harvard Business School Press, 1992).

Chapter 3

1. Richard Luecke, *Scuttle your ships before advancing: And other lessons from history on leadership and change for today's managers* (New York: Oxford University Press, 1994) p. 7.

2. Michael Maccoby, *The leader* (New York: Simon & Schuster, 1981) p. 221.

3. John P. Kotter, *A force for change: How mangement differs from leadership* (New York: Free Press, 1990).

4. John P. Kotter, *The new rules* (New York: The Free Press, 1995) pp. 99–115.

5. Hedrick Smith, *Rethinking America* (New York: Random House, 1995) p. 32.

6. John P. Kotter, *The leadership factor* (New York: The Free Press, 1988) p. 18.

7. See the "Fourteen Points" in W. Edwards Deming, *Out of Crisis* (Cambridge, MA: Massachusetts Institute of Technology/Center for Advanced Engineering Study, 1982) pp. 23–24.

8. V. Daniel Hunt, *Quality in America* (Homewood, IL: BusinessOne Irwin, 1992) p. 9.

9. R.C. Dorney, "Making Time to Manage," *Harvard Business Review,* January–February 1988, p. 39.

10. Walter Kichel III, "A Manager's Career," *Fortune,* April 4, 1994, p. 71.

11. Linda Hill, *Becoming a manager* (Boston, MA: Harvard Business School Press, 1992) p. 211.

Chapter 4

1. Rosabeth Kanter, Globalism/Localism: A New Human Resources Agenda, *Harvard Business Review,* March–April 1991, pp. 9–10.

2. When the dust of the reorganization had settled, all of the personnel affected had found employment, over 65 percent within Johnson & Johnson.

3. Louis S. Richman, "America's Tough New Job Market," *Fortune,* February 24, 1992, p. 52.

4. Robert H. Waterman, Jr., Judith A. Waterman, and Betsy A. Collard, "Toward a Career-Resilient Workforce," *Harvard Business Review,* July–August 1994, p. 87.

INDEX